Ministering
Cross-Culturally

Ministering
Cross-Culturally

An Incarnational Model for Personal Relationships

Second Edition

Sherwood G. Lingenfelter
and Marvin K. Mayers

Baker Academic

A Division of Baker Book House Co
Grand Rapids, Michigan 49516

© 1986, 2003 by Sherwood G. Lingenfelter and Marvin K. Mayers

Published by Baker Academic
a division of Baker Book House Company
P.O. Box 6287, Grand Rapids, MI 49516-6287
www.bakeracademic.com

Second printing, September 2004

Printed in the United States of America

Library of Congress Cataloging-in-Publication Data
Lingenfelter, Sherwood G.
    Ministering cross-culturally : an incarnational model for personal relationships / Sherwood G. Lingenfelter and Marvin K. Mayers.— 2nd ed.
        p.   cm.
    Includes bibliographical references (p.) and index.
    ISBN 0-8010-2647-4 (pbk.)
    1. Missions—Anthropological aspects. 2. Intercultural communi-cation—Religious aspects—Christianity. I. Mayers, Marvin Keene, 1927– II. Title
BV2603.L434 2003
266'.001—dc21   2003043656

To
Ray Chandler,
who, after forty years of missionary service,
continues to seek ways in which to serve his Lord.
Ray, at eighty years of age,
volunteered his services
to the School of Intercultural Studies
at Biola University,
learned how to use a computer,
and keyboarded the original text and revisions
of this book.

For we are God's workmanship, created in Christ Jesus to do good works, which God prepared in advance for us to do.

Ephesians 2:10

Contents

Preface

The subject of this book is the tension and conflict that missionaries, pastors, and laypersons experience when they attempt to work with people who come from different cultural and social backgrounds. The vehicle employed to explore this issue is a model of basic values that points to personal and cross-cultural roots of tension in interpersonal relationships and assists individuals in mastering such tension. The model was developed by Marvin Mayers and first published in 1974 in his *Christianity Confronts Culture*. It grew out of his experience as a missionary with Wycliffe Bible Translators in Guatemala, as an educator at Wheaton College, and as a trainer in cross-cultural ministries with Wycliffe. Since 1974, Mayers has extensively refined the model and further elaborated on its application in Christian ministries.

Sherwood Lingenfelter is the primary author of this book and the source of the various personal reminiscences it contains.

He first became acquainted with Mayers and the model of basic values at the Summer Institute of Linguistics in Norman, Oklahoma, in 1975. Using the model to analyze his own extensive experience in the Pacific islands, Lingenfelter found that it very effectively explained the complex problems of social relationships he had observed in his field work as a cultural anthropologist. After 1975 he served in various fields with Wycliffe Bible Translators as an anthropology consultant for translation and other related ministries. In these diverse assignments, he used the model of basic values to understand conflicts between missionaries and nationals and between one missionary and another.

Following this field service, Lingenfelter went to Biola University in 1983 to prepare students for cross-cultural ministry. He used the model of basic values to help them understand interpersonal conflicts between individuals from the same and different cultures. The students responded so enthusiastically that he began to present the model outside the university setting in various churches in Southern California. Members of these churches found the model helpful in clarifying problems between them and their friends and coworkers in the community, between husbands and wives, and between coworkers in the church. From the success of these presentations in various churches grew the idea for this book. Because Lingenfelter is so heavily indebted to Mayers for the model and for criticism and development of the manuscript, Mayers is named as coauthor.

The key purpose in working with the model of basic values is to equip people to follow what Scripture says about how Christians should relate to others. This volume examines various scriptural materials to see what they teach about relationships. It then explores how these scriptural principles can be applied in concrete behavior as people relate to others in diverse cultural settings.

We intend to make it clear that individuals—the work of God's creative activity—differ greatly in their values and orientations, as do the societies of which they are members. Each society rewards and punishes individuals in accord with its own particular biases. Therefore, persons called to minister in a foreign setting must be acutely aware of the cultural differences they will encounter. By helping readers identify their own value biases, we hope to create in them an increased sensitivity to others. Further, we challenge our readers to adapt their personal lifestyles to build effective bridges of communication with those in their communities who are in need. Throughout the book we attempt to discern from Scripture principles for effective Christian ministry and to draw from those principles applications for the daily realities of interpersonal relationships.

While this book is targeted generally at individuals who expect to engage in cross-cultural ministry, such ministry is to be understood as any ministry in which one interacts with people who have grown up learning values and lifestyle patterns that are different from one's own. In today's world, cross-cultural ministry includes not only people going as missionaries to Latin America, Africa, or Asia but also those who are trying to be effective witnesses in the major urban centers of our country. For example, the members of an adult Sunday school class in a church in Whittier, California, may be as engaged in cross-cultural ministry as people who go to Asia or Latin America. Consider as evidence the fact that in the records of Whittier hospitals alone, more than twenty languages have been listed as the principal language of a patient. Further, Los Angeles has one of the largest Hispanic populations in the world.

Cross-cultural ministry, then, is something in which many thousands of ordinary American Christians will engage. In colleges and Sunday school classes across the United States, people have found the model of basic values to be a significant tool for understanding others in their own community and even for clarifying the tensions that exist in their own marriage or other relationships. One young Hispanic student at Biola University who completed a personal profile and listened to class lectures tearfully told us that for years she had felt there was something wrong with her because no one else seemed to share her personal values and lifestyle. She was overwhelmed to find that God had created individuals like her and that many cultures share her personal orientation to life.

Our objective, then, is to help readers gain a deeper understanding of themselves and the people with whom they live and in the process to help them experience a deeper relationship with God and a more fruitful life of love and ministry to others.

The second edition of this book has been substantially revised in chapters 1 and 9 to reflect some of my growth and thinking over the past fifteen years on issues of culture and the gospel. In particular, I have tried to clarify the idea of cultural bias and how it not only blinds us but also imprisons us in our cultures. For the Christian who seeks to serve in another culture, knowing one's cultural bias is essential to effective ministry. Once we have understood the power of our cultural habits over us, we are more ready to call on the spiritual power and freedom we enjoy in Christ to break the habits of our culture, to let go of them, and to enter into another culture to help those people encounter Christ.

The second important change in these two chapters is their focus on our freedom in Christ. One of the most profound changes we experience when we follow Jesus Christ is liberation from the cultural systems of righteousness, which most people embrace with great enthusiasm. Salvation in Christ releases us from the works of righteousness that are required by our culture and empowers us through faith to follow him as we journey into other cultures, with their conflicting identities and values. As we engage in incarnational ministry, taking on the identities and values of others, we have the opportunity to point others to freedom in Christ.

I want to note a significant omission in the first edition of this work and give special thanks to Stephen O'Brien, who developed the short form of the basic values questionnaire for this book. This short form was extracted from a much longer questionnaire that Marv Mayers used at Biola University.

one

God's Metaphor for Ministry: The Incarnation

In 1967, my wife and I and our two-year-old daughter flew from western New York State to the Pacific islands. We landed on Guam, spent a couple days there, and then flew to Yap, a small island in the western Caroline Islands of Micronesia. For Americans, Yap is geographically in the middle of nowhere. It is almost a thousand miles from the nearest major nation, the Philippines, and in most other directions, thousands of miles of ocean separate it from the rest of the world. It was here that we were to make our home for the next two years.

This began what has become a lifelong adventure for us in cross-cultural living, research, and relationships. I was a graduate student at the time, and our goal was to live in and learn about Yapese culture in preparation for my doctoral dissertation on the impact of twenty years of American administration on the Yapese and their culture. We were young and filled with ideals, and our hope was to apply this learning experience in a life of service to cross-cultural missions and ministry.

Many years have passed now, and as we reflect on that experience, we have a much deeper understanding of our failures and our achievements. The Yapese taught us as much about ourselves as they did about their own culture. The experience of learning was often painful and never easy, but out of those years we developed a new comprehension of who we are and how we can live and work more effectively with others in a culturally diverse world.

The objective of this book is to share some of the conflicts and struggles we experienced and to explore their meaning for the larger issues of cross-cultural living, work, and ministry. To do this we must go beyond specific personal experiences to the underlying principles of culture and communication through which we establish and maintain interpersonal relationships. The particular focus of this book is on priorities or values people use to order their lives and relationships with others. We will explore by means of both a questionnaire concerning basic values and case studies how people within the same culture and in different cultures define standards and establish personal priorities that are often in conflict with those of others. Conflict arises not only from personal and cultural differences but also from the fact that people often attribute moral force to their priorities for personal behavior and judge those who differ from them as flawed, rebellious, or immoral. Personal judgments shared by many become social judgments, and society coerces individuals to follow its value system. Our goal is to help readers arrive at solutions to these conflicts and to suggest ways in which people moving within and across social and cultural boundaries can adapt to and draw on values different from their own.

A central thesis of this book is that the Bible speaks to all people and all cultures and that Jesus Christ is the only faithful example of divine love in interpersonal relationships and communication. Jesus is God with us—the reality of the love of God in human experience. As we explore situations of interpersonal conflict, we will continually return to Scripture to seek principles on which we can build more effective relationships and ministry within and beyond the boundaries of our homogeneous churches and communities. At the same time, we will use insights from the social and behavioral sciences to pose new questions and to develop new perspectives from which to understand more fully the implications of biblical truth. By focusing initially on cross-cultural experiences, we will be forced to examine our basic assumptions about life and to question every aspect of our relationships.

Jesus: The 200-Percent Person

When we arrived on Yap in 1967, the first question we faced was where to live. A Yapese man took me to his village and showed me two locations where I could build a house. One piece of land was situated on an isolated section of beach with a beautiful view of a lagoon and a coral reef. The other was in the midst of several houses where children littered their yards with empty cans and the voices and activities of mothers and children created a cacophony of sound from morning until night. Where should we live? The isolated beach was the dream spot that all middle-class Americans see in their fantasies of South Sea life. The lot in the village had all the characteristics that middle-class America tries to avoid—noise, litter, lack of privacy, and strange people all around. When I naturally chose the beach, my guide said gently to me, "If you want to learn to speak our language, the other place is better for you." His words broke my romantic reverie and challenged my personal interpretation of the right way to live. With a twinge of sadness, I admitted he was right and agreed to the village location. As I expected, the place was noisy, littered, and public, but he was absolutely correct; within a year we had all learned to speak the language.

My experience in this village on Yap gave me a deeper grasp of what John meant when he wrote in his Gospel, "The Word became flesh and made his dwelling among us" (John 1:14). We hold the incarnation as a fundamental doctrine of the Christian faith: God himself became flesh and dwelt among humans. We seldom ask, however, what the implications of this incarnation are. What did it mean for God to become flesh? How did God plan and choose to live among us? In what manner did he come? Does his example have any significance for us as we are sent to others?

The first significant fact about the incarnation is that Jesus came as a helpless infant. In Luke 2:7, we read that he was born as Mary's child, wrapped in swaddling clothes, and placed in a manger. It is noteworthy that God did not come as a fully developed adult, he did not come as an expert, he did not come as a ruler, or even as part of a ruling family or a dominant culture. He was an infant, born into a humble family in a conquered and subjugated land.

The second significant fact about the incarnation is that Jesus was a learner. He was not born with a knowledge of language or culture. In this respect, he was an ordinary child. He learned language from his parents. He learned how to play from his peers. He learned the trade of a carpenter from Joseph and studied the Scriptures and worshiped in the same manner as did all young men of his time. In Luke 2:46, we read that Mary and Joseph found Jesus in the temple, listening to the teachers of the law and asking them questions. This is a profound statement: The Son of God was sitting in the temple, listening and questioning!

The implications of Jesus' status as a learner are seldom discussed, let alone understood or applied. God's Son studied the language, the culture, and the lifestyles of his people for thirty years before he began his ministry. He knew all about their family lives and problems. He stood at their side as learner and as coworker. He learned to read and study the

Scriptures in his local synagogue and earned respect to the point that the people called him Rabbi. He worshiped with them in their synagogues and observed the annual Passover and other feasts in the temple in Jerusalem. He identified totally with those to whom he was sent, calling himself the Son of man. Luke 2:52 tells us that he grew in favor not only with God but with man as well.

The point is that Jesus was a 200-percent person. Philippians 2:6–7 tells us that Jesus was "in very nature God." He was and is 100 percent God. Yet Paul tells us that Jesus took "the very nature of a servant, being made in human likeness." He was 100 percent human. When he spoke of himself, he called himself the Son of man, identifying completely with those to whom he was sent. Let us move our thinking one step further. Jesus was more than simply human; he was also 100 percent Jew. The Samaritan woman in John 4 identified him as such, and he accepted this identification at face value. (Note by contrast that when people tried to make him a king, he resisted.) His disciples and even the Jewish leaders often reminded him of his Jewishness and its attendant cultural obligations (ritual washings, Sabbath observance, avoidance of unclean people and places, etc.). At the crucifixion, Pilate had inscribed over Jesus' head the words "King of the Jews." In sum, he was 100 percent God and 100 percent Jew—a 200-percent person.

Cultural Context

Culture is the anthropologist's label for the sum of the distinctive characteristics of a people's way of life. All human behavior occurs within particular cultures, within socially defined contexts. For example, in America, worship occurs in a specific context with distinctive characteristics. A church building, chairs or pews, music, readings from the Bible, a sermon, an offering, and prayers are all part of that context. The social organization of worship includes pastors, musicians, ushers, a seating arrangement by families, and a schedule of activities. If one were to go to Saudi Arabia, the context of worship would differ dramatically. The mosque would have no chairs, musicians, Bible, or sermon. Removing one's shoes, kneeling, prostration, and prayer would be the primary elements of worship. The sexes are carefully separated, and leaders and learning have only minimal significance. A Moslem entering an American church would not understand what happens there as worship. He may even deny that worship is possible in such a context.

Culture, then, is the conceptual design, the definitions by which people order their lives, interpret their experiences, and evaluate the behavior of others. A Moslem sees men and women sitting together and interprets this as sexual behavior. He evaluates such a situation by comparing it with his past experiences in his own culture. By definition, the commingling of the sexes cannot be part of the context he calls worship. Therefore, to a Moslem, what happens in American churches is not worship. Similarly distinctive definitions, rules, and values are specific to each socially defined context, and these specifics make up the conceptual designs or culture in accordance with which all of us live.

It is fairly obvious, then, that communication requires effective use of contextual cues. When a Moslem removes his shoes as he enters a mosque, it is a cue that he intends to worship there. A cultural cue is a specific signal or sign that people use to communicate the meaning of their behavior. Each culture has literally thousands of cues that signal a change of context and a corresponding need to follow the rules appropriate to the new context.

On Yap, an invitation to chew betel nut is a cue to initiate conversation. This cue is equivalent to offering a cup of coffee in the United States. In the States, guests terminate a conversation by suggesting they must leave, whereas on Yap the host terminates the conversation by saying that it is all right for the guests to leave. A failure to grasp the meaning of such cues results in misunderstandings, confusion, and oftentimes interpersonal conflict.

Personal Culture

One reason it is necessary, even within our own families, to keep the goal of incarnation in view are the differences in our personal standards and ways of life. These personal differences arise out of our unique genetic heritage and individual histories. Each one of us is born into a particular social context and family. It is within that context that we are socialized, or acquire what might be seen as our personal cultural heritage. For our purposes here, cultural heritage is the early learning a child unquestioningly accepts. This learning generally takes place before one is able to enter into dialog with one's parents and make choices by conscious reasoning.

A human being is completely helpless at birth and lives through a period of near-total dependency on others that lasts almost six years. During this time, a child is subjected to the intensive influence of parents and a few other adults. During this intensive interaction, parents seek to teach the child certain forms of behavior, values, and modes of living. They do so through the process of reward or punishment, giving or withholding love. The child's personal temperament is also a factor. While the parents attempt to teach specific patterns of behavior, the child's temperament will to some extent counter the parents' teaching so that what they desire to pass on is rarely if ever accepted in full. Most parents will attest to the fact that children in the same family rarely share the same basic outlook on life, the same patterns of temperament, or the same values and goals. The personalities of children vary. In addition, parents revamp their goals and methods of child rearing as time passes. As a consequence, each child emerges from childhood with a unique personal heritage.

Furthermore, every individual goes through a lifelong process of learning or what anthropologists call enculturation. This larger process is the means by which an individual acquires the cultural heritage of a larger community. For children, this involves peer pressure and peer socialization, learning in school and in play activities. By this time, the learning involves conscious dialog both with adults and with one's peers, and this dialog results in conflict and questioning as well as acceptance. In becoming more independent of one's parents, a child is increasingly influenced by persons outside the immediate family. The child develops an ability to choose what to accept and what to reject. At this point, peer-group influence becomes increasingly important in the child's life. As the child is exposed to new ideas and has an opportunity to select from among them, his or her choices are tempered by feedback from others who either accept or reject him or her. Through that acceptance or rejection the child begins to formulate a conception of his or her own world, a personal culture. The individual will then tend to congregate with those who share similar ideas and interests and avoid those who do not, thus reinforcing his or her own personal choices.

Our personal culture as individuals, then, is unique; it is not the same as that of our parents or of any other individual. It is the product of the combination of (1) the personal cultural heritage acquired through socialization with our parents, (2) the broader cultural heritage acquired through enculturation and feedback from the community, and (3) our act of accepting or rejecting those forces. Each individual develops a personal lifestyle and a set of standards and values by which to order and organize his or her life.

Shared Culture

In spite of the fact that we are all unique persons, we share common beliefs, values, and a way of life with many others around us. We not only share those beliefs but also reinforce them in one another and teach them to our children. The shared aspects of our personal cultures produce the common values, priorities, and standards for behavior that we apply in each social context. We begin to learn these things as helpless infants, and by the time we are adults, they shape much of what we are and do.

This shared culture has great value for us. Because of it, we are able to plan a career with a reliable expectation that we can actually accomplish what we envision. We are able to establish a family and friendships and to fulfill our mutual obligations to one another. When we find ourselves in situations of conflict with others, the standards and procedures of our shared culture furnish mechanisms for settling those disputes, and while the solutions are not always satisfying, the process is familiar and somewhat predictable.

In their collective sum, our personal cultures have enough in common with one another that outsiders look at us and see us as being alike, even though we find great differences among ourselves. These similarities may be reinforced by an institutional identity. We are Americans, not because we are identical but rather because international custom defines nationality by one's place of birth. Other parts of our identity we derive from our race, language, and the groups into which we are born or with which we affiliate during our lives. The groups and institutions of which we are a part coerce us to conform to standards shared by a majority of their members. We learn these rules so that they become natural to us, and we assume that exceptions to our behavior are unnatural and illegitimate. Acceptance in our groups comes at the cost of exclusion from the groups of others. An attempt to belong to groups whose standards are in conflict with ours produces emotional stress within us and antagonism in our relationships with others. For this reason, most of us choose to belong only to those groups within which we find people who have standards and values similar to our own.

As a consequence of our choices, the communities we form include some and exclude others. These social arrangements become an important part of our shared culture. We include those people who reaffirm our values and relationships, and we exclude those who in some way do not measure up to our standards or do not fit within our prescribed sphere of social relationships. This pattern of inclusion and exclusion often prompts us to fear and even reject the very people we are sent to serve.

Culture is always learned and shared with others, and in this process, people perceive and respond to one another in culturally conditioned ways. Edward Hall (1976, 85) suggests that this is useful to us, because it allows us to screen out information that is not essential and protects us from emotional and intellectual overload. Further, it allows us to predict, to some extent, the behavior of others in our own culture. At the same time, the screening process produces a blindness to cues from cultures not our own. A Moslem cannot accept a Christian church service as worship, nor can a Christian accept a Moslem's prayer in a mosque as worship. This cultural blindness makes us ineffective communicators in alien contexts and leads us to assume that the problem lies with others rather than with ourselves.

The cultural bias we share with others in our communities becomes a consensus we use to protect ourselves from others. Through this consensus, we regulate the behavior of our members and reject those who refuse to conform. We become certain that our way of doing things is the proper way, and we are blinded to the possibilities of doing things differently or of engaging in new behaviors that might be beneficial to our community. Our very agreement becomes a distortion of the reality of our experience, a defense against other peoples and other ways of life. The comfort of our community becomes a bias toward others and a blindness to viable relationships different from our own.

It is because of cultural blindness that we must become incarnate in the culture and thus in the lives of the people we wish to serve. We must begin as a child and grow in their midst. We must be learners and let them teach us before we can hope to teach them and introduce them to the master Teacher.

The practice of incarnation (i.e., a willingness to learn as if we were helpless infants) is the first essential step toward breaking this pattern of excluding others. Missionaries, by the nature of their task, must become personally immersed with people who are different. To follow the example of Christ, that of incarnation, means undergoing drastic personal reorientation. They must be socialized all over again into a new cultural context. They must enter a culture as if they were children—ignorant of everything, from the customs of eating and talking to the patterns of work, play, and worship. Moreover, they must do this in the spirit of Christ, that is, without sin. While most of us may not face situations requiring such total reorientation, the incarnation principle can also be applied effectively in family and church life.

A Personal Inventory

Take an inventory of the various cultural labels that apply to you. You might be, for example, 100 percent German, English, Italian, or American. You might also be classified as a 100-percent southerner, easterner, or mid-westerner and more specifically as an Arizonian, Californian, or New Yorker. Theologically, you might be evangelical, fundamental, or liberal; denominationally, Baptist, Presbyterian, Lutheran, Brethren, or Free Church.

When I arrived on Yap, I was a Pennsylvanian-born preacher's kid who had learned to say "Yes, sir" and "Yes, ma'am" in Virginia, who had enjoyed Charles Dickens and Mendelssohn's *Elijah* with black classmates in Ohio, who had been a "brave son" at Wheaton College and had married a "daughter true." I had received excellent Christian teaching, was licensed as a Grace Brethren elder, and had been trained at the University of Pittsburgh by internationally renowned anthropologists. I was clearly a 100-percent middle-class, evangelical American. I was definitely not Yapese!

What kind of persons should we be when we enter alien cultures? We can find some direct instructions in Scripture. In Philippians 2:5, Paul says, "Your attitude should be the same as that of Christ Jesus." First Peter 2:21 states, "Christ suffered for you, leaving you an example, that you should follow in his steps." If Jesus did indeed set the example, then it was my responsibility to work as hard to become Yapese as he did to become a Jew. Through the Great Commission, Jesus sends us out into all the world, and as his messengers, we are to follow his example, that is, we are to become incarnate in the cultures to which we are sent.

The World Christian: A 150-Percent Person

The challenge is to become what Malcolm McFee (1968) calls a 150-percent person. McFee uses this concept to describe Black Foot Indians who are enculturated into white American society. He argues that they are still 75-percent traditional Black Foot, but they have also learned to adapt to and follow the larger American culture to the point at which some are 75 percent white as well. He calls these people 150-percent persons. Like these Indians, we will never become 100-percent insiders in another culture or subculture. The only way that is possible is the way Jesus did it, to be born into that other culture and to spend a lifetime in it. However, it is possible to follow his example, to be "imitators of God," as Paul commands in Ephesians 5:1, and to "live a life of love" (v. 2) in the culture in which we hope to minister. Our goal should be to become more than we are; for me it was to become at least part Yapese, even if that meant being less than 100 percent American.

To become a 150-percent person is more than an ordinary challenge. Discarding or setting aside something of one's Americanness or one's social or church identity is almost sacrilege to many people. Our way of life is often equated with godliness, and we defend vigorously its apparent rightness. As such, this way of life has become our prison. We forget the example set by Christ, who, "being in very nature God," did not cling to that identity but instead became not only a Jew but also a servant among Jews (Phil. 2:6–7). We must love the people to whom we minister so much that we are willing to enter their culture as children, to learn how to speak as they speak, play as they play, eat what they eat, sleep where they sleep, study what they study, and thus earn their respect and admiration. In essence, we must leave our prison, enter their prison, and become full participants within it.

The excitement of becoming 50 percent Yapese was one of the highlights of my life. I will never forget the ecstasy of my first complete conversation in the Yapese language or the deep admiration I felt upon grasping their custom of sharing their personal possessions. I also remember the anxiety when I felt unwanted or burdensome to my host, the isolation when my speech was so poor that people did not want to be bothered by me, and the frustration and boredom I felt with the hours of what seemed to be trivial conversation. The lesson here is that becoming incarnate in another culture will be a trial by fire, a test of inner strength, of personal faith, and most of all a test of the veracity of one's love. An individual who is not ready to give up being an American for a time and to begin learning as a child is not ready for the challenge of cross-cultural ministry.

If we are to follow the example of Christ, we must aim at incarnation! Jesus said, "If anyone would come after me, he must deny himself" (Matt. 16:24). These acts of self-denial are in fact the first steps of freedom in Christ. We must consciously release our attachments to home, income security, convenience, significance in work or ministry, and even comfort of family. We must enter a new community of strangers, often without many if not most of the comforts and symbols of home, and begin as children, learning at the feet of those we have gone to serve. We must be willing to become world Christians. The challenges will shape us; the changes will trouble us. Our bodies will get sick, our minds will suffer fatigue, our emotions will sweep us from ecstasy to depression. Yet the love of Christ will sustain us so that we can identify with Paul, who said, "I have become all things to all men so that by all possible means I might save some. I do all this for the sake of the gospel, that I may share in its blessings" (1 Cor. 9:22–23).

two

A Model of Basic Values

The first step in the process of incarnation is learning the language. For most missionaries, learning a second language is a difficult and consuming challenge. Language school usually occupies the first year of a missionary term, and that schooling only begins the process of language learning. Fluency is generally two or three more years down the road.

Many people mistakenly believe that when they have finally mastered a language, they have also learned the corresponding culture. The tragedy is that because they operate with this misconception, they never learn what Edward Hall calls the silent language of culture. He observes that language is but one of ten primary message systems found in every culture (1973, 38–59). The others are temporality (attitude toward time, routine, and schedule), territoriality (attitude toward space and property), exploitation (methods of control, attitude toward the use and sharing of resources), association (family, kin, and community), subsistence (attitude toward work and division of labor), bisexuality (differing modes of speech, dress, and conduct), learning (by observation, modeling, or instruction), play (humor and games), and defense (health procedures, social conflicts, and beliefs). Each message system has rules that govern relationships and communication; each has a structure, a pattern, and variations that must be learned. Knowing a language, therefore, opens up only roughly one-tenth of what one could learn about a lifestyle, a culture.

Furthermore, language itself is, in effect, a vast oversimplification of the world around us. For example, when we talk about "a chair," we have an image in our minds. However, that single lexical category covers a vast quantity of different objects. The particular objects in our experience can be identified only by the use of modifiers such as red, yellow, folding, molded, wooden, plastic, reclining, and rocking. Language, then, does not communicate a specific reality or experience but only a conceptual model of that which we experience.

A Model to Understand Culture

The purpose of this book is to examine experiences in interpersonal relations, using a conceptual model that will provide an understanding of our underlying priorities or values and those of the people with whom we interact. It is important to understand that when we talk about a model, we are talking about something that approximates reality. A model of an airplane is not an airplane. A model of a house is not a house. The model of values presented here is an approximate representation of priorities; it is not a definitive explanation of experience. It should also be kept in mind that these priorities, which identify what is more important and what is less important in one's experience, may be unique to a person or may be shared and thus reflect the cultural values of a group.

The model of basic values, which was first proposed by Marvin Mayers (1974), contains twelve key elements. These elements are presented in the form of six pairs of contrasting traits. Each pair may be viewed as opposite poles on a continuum or plotted on a more complex matrix. The remaining chapters probe the distinguishing characteristics of each basic value and explore the complex tensions that arise as people and cultures actualize one or many of these priorities in social behavior.

The model of basic values will, like language, produce an oversimplification of the reality of our experience. But at the same time, it should help us understand something about that reality, just as when we talk about "a chair" we distinguish that object from a couch, an airplane, and other dissimilar objects. We can communicate essential ideas about our experience in such a way that others with the same language can understand generally what we are talking about.

To help you get a better grasp of how insights from the model may be applied to your own life and ministry, we encourage you to plot your own personal profile. To aid in that process, a questionnaire has been included. It is best to complete the questionnaire before reading further; in this way, there will be less temptation to slant your profile to your expectations.

Basic Values Questionnaire

Determine to what extent each of the following statements describes your thinking and approach to life. If the statement is *not at all* descriptive of you, write the number 1 in the blank space. If it is *very* descriptive of you, write the number 7. Write the number 4 if the statement describes you only somewhat. Use the number 2 or 3 for items that are less descriptive of you and the number 5 or 6 for those that are more descriptive. Respond to all statements with a number from 1 to 7.

_____ 1. I would not feel comfortable working for a large company because I would never see the whole picture of what I was working on.

_____ 2. I seek out friends and enjoy talking about any subject that happens to come up.

_____ 3. I avoid setting goals for fear that I might not reach them.

_____ 4. I am more concerned about what I have accomplished than I am with the position and title of my job.

_____ 5. I seldom think much about the future; I just like to get involved in things as they turn up.

_____ 6. I feel things are either right or wrong; discussion of "gray" areas makes me uncomfortable and seems to compromise the truth.

_____ 7. When making a decision, I feel that more than one of the options can be a right choice.

_____ 8. When I set a goal, I dedicate myself to reaching that goal, even if other areas of my life suffer as a result of it.

_____ 9. I am always one of the first to try something new.

_____ 10. I tend to associate only with people of the same social status.

_____ 11. I feel strongly that time is a scarce commodity, and I value it highly.

_____ 12. When my car needs tuning, I go to the dealer rather than let my neighbor who works out of his garage do the job. With professionals I know it will be done right.

_____ 13. I like performing before an audience because it pushes me to perform better.

_____ 14. My primary criteria for buying a car are low price and a record of quality and reliability; I do not let family or friends influence me to spend more for a "name brand."

_____ 15. My desk or work area is very organized. There is a place for everything, and everything is in its place.

_____ 16. I attend lectures and read books by experts to find solutions to issues of importance to me.

_____ 17. If offered a promotion that entailed moving to another city, I would not be held back by relationships with parents and friends.

_____ 18. I find it difficult to relate to people who have a significantly higher occupational or social position than mine.

_____ 19. I always wear a watch and refer to it regularly in order not to be late for anything.

_____ 20. I feel very frustrated if someone treats me like a stereotype.

_____ 21. I tend not to worry about potential problems; I wait until a problem develops before taking action.

_____ 22. When waiting in line, I tend to start up conversations with people I do not know.

_____ 23. I hate to arrive late; sometimes I stay away rather than walk in late.

_____ 24. I get annoyed at people who want to stop a discussion and push the group to make a decision, especially when everyone has not had a chance to express his or her opinion.

_____ 25. I plan my daily and weekly activities. I am annoyed when my schedule or routine gets interrupted.

_____ 26. I do not take sides in a discussion until I have heard all the arguments.

_____ 27. Completing a task is almost an obsession with me, and I cannot be content until I am finished.

_____ 28. I enjoy breaking out of my routine and doing something totally different every now and then to keep life exciting.

_____ 29. When involved in a project, I tend to work on it until completion, even if that means being late on other things.

_____ 30. I eat in only a few select public places outside my home where I can be sure the food is the best quality and I can find the specific items I enjoy.

_____ 31. Even though I know it might rain, I would attend a friend's barbecue rather than excuse myself to repair the damage a storm has done to my roof.

_____ 32. I always submit to the authority of my boss, pastor, and teachers, even if I feel they may be wrong.

_____ 33. I feel there is a standard English grammar and that all Americans should use it.

_____ 34. To make meals more interesting, I introduce changes into the recipes I find in cookbooks.

_____ 35. I argue my point to the end, even if I know I am wrong.

_____ 36. I do not feel that anything I have done in the past matters much; I have to keep proving myself every day.

_____ 37. When starting a new job, I work especially hard to prove myself to my fellow workers.

_____ 38. When introducing important people, I usually include their occupation and title.

_____ 39. I talk with others about my problems and ask them for advice.

_____ 40. I avoid participating in games at which I am not very good.

_____ 41. Even if in a hurry while running errands, I will stop to talk with a friend.

_____ 42. I have set specific goals for what I want to accomplish in the next year and the next five years.

_____ 43. I like to be active with many things so that at any one time I have a choice of what to do.

_____ 44. When shopping for a major item, I first get expert advice and then buy the recommended item at the nearest reasonable store.

_____ 45. I enjoy looking at art and trying to figure out what the artist was thinking and trying to communicate.

_____ 46. I feel uncomfortable and frustrated when a discussion ends without a clear resolution of the issue; nobody wins the argument.

_____ 47. I resist a scheduled life, preferring to do things on the spur of the moment.

_____ 48. When leading a meeting, I make sure it begins and ends on time.

Analysis of Answers

To determine your personal profile, fill in your response to each of the corresponding statements in the questionnaire. (If, for example, your response to statement 1 was 5, enter 5 in the first space after "Holistic thinking.") Then add the five numbers in each line and divide the total by five to obtain your average score for each trait.

						Total	Average
1. Time orientation	11	19	23	25	48		
2. Event orientation	5	24	29	31	47		
3. Dichotomistic thinking	6	10	15	33	46		
4. Holistic thinking	1	7	20	26	45		
5. Crisis orientation	6	12	16	30	44		
6. Noncrisis orientation	7	9	21	34	43		
7. Task orientation	8	12	17	27	42		
8. Person orientation	2	39	22	31	41		
9. Status focus	10	18	32	33	38		
10. Achievement focus	4	14	20	36	37		
11. Concealment of vulnerability	3	23	32	35	40		
12. Willingness to expose vulnerability	9	13	28	34	39		

Personal Profile

On each axis, find your average score for that orientation. Then plot on each grid the point where the two average scores intersect. This point indicates your basic tendency.

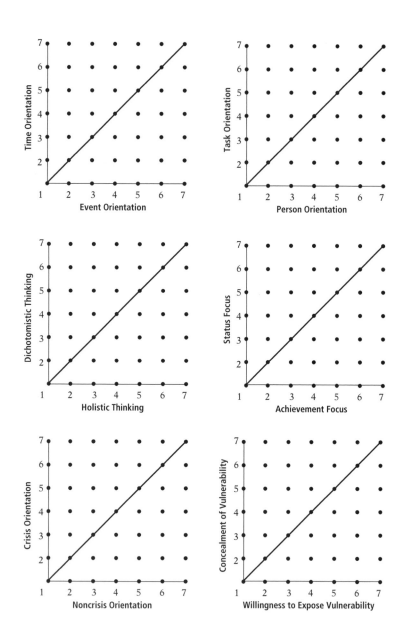

The personal profile of basic traits is an approximate representation of the motivations behind an individual's actions within his or her culture. The matrix form presents the contrasting traits as concurrent forces pulling in different (but not necessarily opposite) directions. The scores on each matrix indicate the relative strength of each particular trait as one makes decisions and interacts with others. A score of (2,6) on the first grid (i.e., event has a priority rating of 2, time a rating of 6) suggests that the constraints of time exert a far stronger pull on the decisions and actions of the individual than does commitment to completion of the events in which he or she participates. A score of (2,2) probably means that neither trait is exerting a strong influence.

The personal profile of basic values can be applied in several ways: (1) It can serve as the basis of a judgment against a person who does not behave as we would wish; (2) it can serve as a radar signal that we are headed for conflict with another person and thus should avoid confrontation; (3) it can serve as an insight that will help us achieve maximum intelligent interaction with another person. In the chapters that follow, we will see that by carefully choosing our responses to people and cultures whose orientations differ from ours, we can reduce or even resolve tensions in interpersonal relations.

three

Tensions about Time

The building of the Yap Evangelical Church was used for two services each Sunday morning. A Palauan-language service began at half past eight, and a Yapese service followed at eleven. On one particular Sunday, the senior pastor and head of the churches of Palau had come to Yap to speak to the local Palauan congregation. Because of the special nature of the service, he was not finished when it came time for the Yapese service at eleven. A dear German sister, veteran of thirty years on Yap and Palau, bustled around impatiently at the bottom of the hill until she could contain herself no longer. Abruptly she ordered a Yapese girl to go up and ring the bell. Needless to say, the Palauan pastor was deeply embarrassed; he quickly closed his sermon, and the Palauan congregation rushed out of the church. When the Yapese pastor realized what had happened, he was mortified and apologized to the Palauan pastor and people as they came out. Then during the Yapese service he publicly rebuked the sister in a very gentle way, saying, "We Yapese don't care when the service begins; we are happy to wait until our Palauan brothers are finished. For us time doesn't matter; we just want our Palauan brothers to enjoy their fellowship here in our church." A half hour was not important to the Yapese congregation. They would have waited two hours without feeling imposed upon or becoming angry. Americans and Germans, on the contrary, have a very short time-fuse and experience anxiety when there is a delay of five or more minutes.

The concept of being late varies significantly from one culture to the next and from one individual to the next. I can recall waiting in the car for my wife outside the library of the state university where she worked; invariably she was late. If she was only five minutes late, I excused her without hesitation. However, sometimes she was as much as fifteen minutes late, and on those occasions I greeted her with a demand for an explanation, thus producing tension between us. On a few rare occasions she was as much as twenty to thirty minutes late, and I must confess that I was enraged to have been kept waiting for so long. On those occasions communication between us was nearly impossible because of the hostility the long wait had aroused in me.

Yapese people would find my anger unacceptable and quite puzzling. In their scheme of things, one is not late even if he or she arrives two hours after the appointed time. Missionaries who have worked in Latin America report a similar attitude there, although the Latin American definition of "late" entails a shorter period than does that of the Yapese. Most North Americans will begin to experience tension when others are fifteen minutes late; most Latin Americans will experience tension when others are more than one hour late; Yapese will not experience tension until the expected party is about three hours late.

Marvin Mayers suggests that Americans and Germans belong to time-oriented cultures, whereas Latin American and Yapese cultures are more event-oriented. People who are time-oriented express great concern about punctuality, the length of time expended, and utilization of time to its maximum potential. People who are event-oriented show concern that an activity be completed regardless of the length of time required and emphasize unscheduled participation rather than carefully structured activities.

Table 1

Concepts of Lateness

	Lateness Excused	Tension	Hostility
Yapese	2 hours	3 hours	4 hours
Latin American	1/2 hour	1 hour	2 hours
North American	5 minutes	15 minutes	1/2 hour

To gain an understanding of the characteristics of time and event orientations, we will examine them first as conceptual opposites. While characteristics of each are extremely different, human behavior rarely falls at either extreme. Rather, most people are caught in a tension between the two poles. In some circumstances, we yield to the pull of one side of the continuum, while in other circumstances, we yield the other way. We speak of time orientation and event orientation to indicate which side of the continuum or matrix dominates individuals and cultures. Each side has many consistent behavioral manifestations.

Consider this illustration. Over a period of several years I participated in candidate-orientation sessions for a mission organization in the United States. The first leader to invite me said that we would gather each day to discuss whatever the candidates or I wanted to discuss but would follow no fixed schedule. We began sometime after breakfast, broke for meals or relaxation, and finished in the afternoon or evening as our interests and ability to concentrate dictated. A few years later another man was given the responsibility for the program. This second leader devised a schedule of forty-five-minute periods with a specific subject matter assigned to each period. These two men illustrate very different types of persons: The first is event-oriented, while the second is clearly time-oriented. Both orientations are valid. Some people, however, are happier when there is no set routine, and others feel more comfortable with a precise schedule. It is noteworthy that two people in the same organization and from the same cultural background had such different ways of dealing with time.

Time-Oriented Persons and Cultures

Time-oriented persons and cultures exhibit a high concern about schedule and punctuality within that schedule, and this concern is manifested in a variety of ways. American schools, businesses, and homes often have a clock in every room, and nearly everyone wears a watch. Each day is organized into time periods of specific length, and the use of each period is carefully planned. Meetings, work periods, and breaks are set by the clock, and individuals carry personal calendars to schedule their activities. For some time-oriented persons, anniversaries, dates, and historical chronologies have special importance.

Another aspect of time orientation involves scheduling toward a goal. Time-oriented persons typically have specific objectives they want to accomplish within a given period. They will set a time within which they must finish a job or carry out a specific activity. People with this orientation often fill their time to its maximum potential. Their lives take on a frantic pace and are so filled with appointments that nothing can be done on the spur of the moment.

In time-oriented cultures, a careful utilization of time is often associated with reward. For example, we may tell a child, "Give yourself twenty minutes to do that assignment. If you push yourself to finish it in that time period, then you will have the entire evening free." My son has always had a difficult time working in this way because by nature he is more event-oriented. He will combine homework with music and play and after three hours will have only four sentences of an assignment written or most of his math still to be done. A personal goal, however, can motivate him to change his pattern of action. On one occasion he wanted to see a movie. I initially said no, but about ten minutes before the movie was scheduled to begin, I said, "Joel, I'm going to the office; I can take you to the movie if you have finished your homework." Within five minutes he was finished. Because he wanted to go to the movie, he was motivated to do his math very quickly. But until he had a particular objective in mind, time was not a critical factor in his thinking. Other people see time as money and use each unit to earn a particular reward or accomplish a particular objective.

Event-Oriented Persons and Cultures

At the other end of the continuum, event-oriented people are concerned more about the details of what is going to happen than about when it begins and when it ends. The event-oriented mission director was concerned about what happened to the candidates in their training, but he did not care when it happened. He had no specific agenda for any of the scheduled sessions. Rather, his primary interest was in what happened in the process of training candidates and whether this experience proved meaningful to them and prepared them to do their jobs more effectively. He was concerned that learning occur, but the schedule we followed and the amount of time we took mattered little to him. Time-oriented people cannot understand this lifestyle, for to them a person can learn only by keeping to a tightly controlled schedule. Any other way of learning is seen as inefficient and conducive to laziness.

Table 2
Time and Event Orientations

Time Orientation	Event Orientation
1. Concern for punctuality and amount of time expended	1. Concern for details of the event, regardless of time required
2. Careful allocation of time to achieve the maximum within set limits	2. Exhaustive consideration of a problem until resolved
3. Tightly scheduled, goal-directed activities	3. A "let come what may" outlook not tied to any precise schedule
4. Rewards offered as incentives for efficient use of time	4. Stress on completing the event as a reward in itself
5. Emphasis on dates and history	5. Emphasis on present experience rather than the past or future

For event-oriented people, it is more important to complete an activity than to observe arbitrary constraints of time.

Baseball is one activity in American culture that still follows event-oriented rules. A ball game has no fixed time limit; it will continue through as many extra innings as necessary. Church services among some ethnic groups (black, Hispanic, Korean) also operate on an event-oriented schedule. They rarely begin on time and frequently last two, three, or more hours.

Event orientation produces a "let come what may" outlook unbound by schedules. Event-oriented persons will often be late to time-structured meetings because the event in which they were previously engaged was not completed on time. For them, meetings begin when the last person arrives and end when the last person leaves. Participation and completion are the central goals. For event-oriented people, playing the game is indeed more important than winning. They also differ in their style of managing problems or crises. Whereas time-oriented people will quickly grow weary of discussion and call for a vote, event-oriented people will exhaustively consider a problem, hearing all issues and deliberating until they reach unanimous agreement.

Finally, for event-oriented people, the present is more important than either the past or the future. History is a matter more of sequence than of exact dates. The Yapese have no idea of their specific birthdates, but they do know the chronological order of the birthdates of everyone in their villages. The issues of history are of little consequence to them; their primary preoccupations are with things that have relevance now.

The Biblical Perspective

It can be argued with reasonable conviction that Jewish culture during the life of Christ was predominantly event-oriented. The concept of *hour* as used in the New Testament was an approximate measure, marked technically on a sundial but reckoned by most people by the general position of the sun in the sky. Daytime was divided into quarters, beginning at dawn, then marked at midmorning, midday, and midafternoon, and ending at sunset. The night was also divided into four parts—the evening, midnight, cockcrowing, and morning watches (Miller, 1983). These time periods were loosely drawn, and the evidence presented in the Gospels suggests little or no concern for punctuality or scheduling.

In fact, the evidence found in the Gospel of John, although meager, suggests that Jesus, incarnate as he was in Jewish culture, was event-oriented in his personal life and ministry. The opening drama of Jesus' ministry reports how two of John the Baptist's disciples came to spend the day with Jesus (John 1:39). It was an unplanned encounter. Some commentators (e.g., Brown 1970) suggest that it may have been late Friday afternoon, and the two men may have had to decide whether to rush home or to spend the entire Sabbath day with Jesus. Whether or not the Sabbath was involved, they abandoned their previous plans in order to enjoy fully this encounter with Christ.

Other texts show a similar disregard for schedule. John 3:2 reports that Nicodemus came to Jesus at night but indicates no displeasure on Jesus' part at giving an interview at such an unusual time. In another incident (John 4:4–42), Jesus, tired from his journey, sat by Jacob's well in Samaria, waiting for his disciples to bring some food. When they finally came back with provisions, Jesus showed no interest in the food but continued his teaching. Because a number of villagers believed in him, he agreed to disregard his plan to continue his journey, and he and the disciples stayed there two more days. Later Jesus received a message that his friend Lazarus was sick. Although he knew Lazarus was already dead and Mary and Martha were grief-stricken, he did not hurry but waited two days before doing anything (John 11:6).

This is not to say that Jesus cared little about time but that he was fully incarnate in the culture of his day. He lived and ministered in a manner common among the Jews. However, when time became important in God's plan, then Jesus pressed others into action. For example, in John 4:35–36,

Jesus rebukes the disciples for neglecting the pressing needs of the people and admonishes them that God's harvesttime is now! In Matthew 4:17, we read that the time had come for Jesus to preach, and in Matthew 16:21, the time had come to explain his suffering, death, and resurrection. Note, however, that "time" as stressed in these texts does not refer to a schedule but to opportunity (McConnell 1983, 61–70).

Implications for Cross-Cultural Ministry

What do these New Testament examples mean for our relationships with others and for our ministry? In our scheme of thought and behavior, are we time-oriented or event-oriented? The case of the two mission leaders described earlier illustrates how people in the same culture may have very different attitudes toward and approaches to time. Often people who are so different become frustrated with one another and even reject one another, to the point that it is impossible for them to work together effectively. When the orientation of an entire culture conflicts with that of a missionary, attempts at cross-cultural communication and ministry may become characterized by hostility and strife.

It is fairly obvious that American culture at large values time orientation. For example, if a movie does not start on time, the audience soon stomps, yells, and hisses as people express anger about the delay. Some people in the audience, however, like the event-oriented mission leader, might not be agitated by the tardiness as much as dismayed at the impatience of their fellow Americans. We can observe similar responses in church and mission activities. If a church retreat is not organized and on schedule, some participants will grumble about wasting time. The event-oriented leader is not following a culturally approved manner of scheduling. In such a case, the demands of American culture for efficient use of time outweigh the personal preferences of any of the participants.

Other cultures are quite different in their orientation toward time. A sharp contrast to American attitudes may be found among Pacific islanders. For example, when we went to see a movie at a local Yap school, people started to assemble at half past eight. An hour later most of the crowd had arrived, yet stragglers came as late as ten. A movie hardly ever started before ten o'clock, even though the leaders may have announced it would begin at nine. These men delayed because not everyone had arrived, and it was only courteous to wait. When they decided to begin the movie, they first had to start the generator, which often took a while. If they had trouble with the generator, they might spend half an hour taking it apart, cleaning the carburetor, and making necessary adjustments. Finally, only after the generator was running did they load the film into the projector. The man who changed the reels worked very leisurely. In fact, he and others often chewed betel nut during the break and talked to one another. Often the movie ended after midnight. If the generator broke down during the film, the Yapese talked, chewed betel nut, and rather enjoyed the occasion. If it proved impossible to restart the generator, they gradually drifted off to their homes. Although they had failed to see the movie, they nevertheless had had an eventful evening.

To be effective in cross-cultural ministry, one must adapt to such differences in the view of time. An American participating in Micronesian activities must expect to encounter a different attitude toward time. If this difference leads to frustration, compensating strategies can be adopted. A simple strategy is to go to an event at one's convenience, not at the announced time. In most cases, the formal activity begins at least two hours after the announced starting time.

There are a number of ways in which the American and Micronesian attitudes toward time differ. First, Americans have a sense of urgency about time. We feel that time is valuable and that it is running out. American young people, particularly, fear that time might pass by before they can experience all of life. We have a sense of urgency about getting a job done and about planning what to do next. We cannot wait until our vacation or the weekend or the last day of school. We focus our attention on the next event. Micronesians, however, do not feel this time pressure. Time to them is not nearly as valuable as we believe it to be.

Another aspect of the American attitude, as Edward Hall points out (1973, 152–55), is the need we feel for variety in our experience. We like to do different things. Americans in Micronesia are often frustrated because they have no place to go. To go out for a drive is to go to the same places, traveling over a system of roads that leads no farther than twenty-five miles from the starting point. Pacific island life offers little variety. While Americans seek change and new experiences, Micronesians are accustomed to monotony and routine. There is little to do on these islands that has not already been done many times before. There are few places to go, and one meets with the same people and follows the same routines over and over again.

Another characteristic of Americans is what Hall (1973, 153) calls monochronism, or single-minded use of time. For example, if I begin a building project, I work on it continuously until I complete it. Then I may move on to writing an article or preparing for a lecture or some other intense activity. I have difficulty doing more than one thing at the same time. Keeping two projects going at once is troublesome for Americans. Many of us prefer to focus our energies on a single activity.

Again, Micronesians tend to differ in this regard. They feel no pressure to get things done. I watched a Yapese man take two years to build a house. He would work on the house for a day or two, then go fishing for a few days to provide protein for his family's diet. Then he might take a few days to help others or to do no work of any kind at all. He was not in a hurry because he did not have winter to worry about, and the place where he was staying gave him shelter from the rain. He wanted a new house, but it was something for which there was little haste.

Discordant Individual Behavior

We have examined how cultures manifest either a time or an event orientation. However, there are individuals in every culture who are at variance with the pattern of the whole. When I surveyed students at the State University of New York College at Brockport, I found that they tended to be event-oriented. This suggests that American college students today are not as time-conscious and as highly motivated to keep a schedule as their culture would want them to be. Students come late to classes, they do not submit their papers on time, and they begin their weekends on Thursday—all of which reflects event orientation. These students are often living in conflict with the expectations of their culture. At times they are frustrated by it, and at times their culture is frustrated by them.

Some have suggested that college students are late with their assignments and generally not committed to keeping a schedule because they consider themselves to be free from rules; they constitute what has been called the "me" generation. Although education in the recent past has placed greater emphasis on individual self-realization, I do not think this explanation is adequate. Children in the same family often have significantly different attitudes toward time. One child does not accept the constraints of time easily but must struggle to learn the discipline of schedule, whereas other children in the same family submit very readily to time constraints. Each child learns to yield on occasion to the demands either of time or event, but the event-oriented child finds the cultural system rankling and must work to adapt to it. On the other hand, time-oriented people may rationalize some of their attitudes with the arguments advanced by their culture, but these are not adequate explanations for their personal behavior. The precise causes of their behavior are probably more complex than anyone understands.

The point is that individuals vary greatly within a culture, and there are no simple explanations for those differences.

As each culture selects and emphasizes its particular values, there are always people who are frustrated. Some Yapese are frustrated by event orientation and find that their attitudes are disapproved of by their culture just as we disapprove of those who deviate from our cultural norms. Some people simply do not fit into their culture because their basic personalities are in some way different.

Unfortunately, many well-meaning Christians label the discordant person as rebellious or carnal. A child may be chided, threatened, and coerced and thus build up deep inner frustration, self-rejection, and a despairing sense of inability to please others and God. An adult may be accused of rebellion or may be denied a useful role in a group primarily because of the frustration others have with his or her attitude toward and utilization of time. The critics fail to see that these same persons may often be out of step because they have taken time to help their neighbor (notice Luke 10:30–37). The qualities that make them poor time-oriented personalities allow them to give other people high priority in their values. We may well wonder how Jesus would have responded to the demands of many church and mission organizations today for detailed weekly or monthly reports. What modern preacher can adjust his schedule and stay an extra two days in a town where people show an unusual interest in his teaching?

God's Priorities

Figure 1 shows that cultures vary greatly in the emphases they assign to time and event. For American culture, which frequently emphasizes the constraints of time over event, the priority rating of the event might reasonably be plotted at 2 and the priority rating of time at 6 (2,6). The Yapese seem almost a mirror opposite culturally, allowing an event almost always to take precedence over time. We may plot Yapese culture at (6,2) on the grid. Koreans and Latin Americans fall somewhere in between these two extremes. Since Korean church services tend to last from two to four hours, which is longer than those of Latin Americans, let us hypothesize that Koreans fall at (5,4) on the grid and Latin Americans at (3,5). Individuals in any of these cultures may vary greatly from these points.

Figure 1

Values Assigned to Time and Event

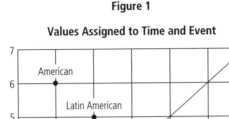

Some might wonder which of these people are more godly in their priorities. To answer this question we must recognize that our way with time is not God's way. In fact, no culture has God's priorities, for in God's scheme the emphases on time and event exist together in complete harmony. William McConnell suggests that time is "a gift from God, and that his priorities can always be fulfilled in the amount of time we have been given. . . . God is lavish with his gifts, so that there is always enough time to do what Jesus calls us to do" (1983, 89). Following this suggestion, we cannot plot God's priorities on the matrix, since God's priorities are not bound by space and time and God's priorities for us meet us at our points of weakness and need. Jesus demonstrated his Father's priority when he went into the wilderness to pray and the crowd pursued him so that he could not get away. Rather than reject them, Jesus gave them his time, healing them, teaching them, and feeding them, and when evening came he sent them away. Only after all their needs had been met did he continue by night into the wilderness, where he prayed alone until he walked on the water to meet his disciples in the fourth (or morning) watch (Matt. 14:13–25). Few of us have the strength or will to follow this example. Jesus attended to the multitude around him, and then he ministered to himself.

An important key to effective cross-cultural ministry is an incarnational attitude toward time and event—we must adapt to the time and event priorities of the people with whom we work. When we Americans enter other cultures, however, we often bring a cultural blindness to this issue. We feel the urgency of time and orient our lives to reflect our own culture. God commands us, however, to do nothing out of self-centeredness but to consider others better than ourselves (Phil. 2:3–5). Our attitude should be the same as that of Christ Jesus, to satisfy the time and event priorities of others before considering our own. With such a goal, we will move toward a more effective ministry to persons whose cultural values are different from our own.

---

four
_____

Tensions Regarding Judgment

After I had learned to speak the Yapese language, I asked some of the old people to tell me stories about the origin of Yap and about Yapese cultural history. As I listened to these accounts, I began to sort them into an integrated whole. One story told about the first family on Yap and how they had settled and had children, who were the founders of the modern clans. Another story told about the great flood that had come to Yap, washing away the central mountain and destroying all of the island except for one family with seven children. The seven all settled in different places and began producing children of their own. I asked, reminiscent of the age-old question as to where Cain got his wife, where these people got their spouses, since they did not marry one another. The Yapese answered that they did not know and that it was not important. They insisted that I did not understand the meaning of the story. I persisted with another line of questioning. The Yapese have about thirty matrilineal clans, and each has a story of its origin. For example, the porpoise clan, the rope clan, and the mushroom clan all have separate accounts of their origins, so I asked how these stories fit with the flood story. My informants shook their heads in despair. "These have nothing to do with the flood story. Why do you insist on putting these things together? They are completely different."

My problem in interviewing the Yapese was that my nature and my training encouraged me to line everything up in rows. I want to have everything sorted, systematically organized, and fitting into its proper place. I like to divide everything into constituent parts and then resort them into a clear pattern. American culture generally rewards this type of thinking.

Science, social science, and theology are all organizing and systematizing disciplines. The Hebrews, however, were not systematic, and apparently as God revealed himself to them, he did not insist that they become so. They expressed their comprehension of God in holistic forms such as independent narratives, life histories, and prophecies. The Old Testament nowhere attempts to put everything together in a systematic way. Someone who likes to see everything in clearly outlined relationships might call the Hebrews disorganized. But they communicated in a holistic style. They did not worry about sorting everything into a comprehensive system; each point was part of a distinctive and separate whole. In contrast, our western, Greco-European tradition seeks an Aristotelian comprehension of the universe, one in which everything fits into a logically cohesive worldview.

When I insisted on combining all the Yapese stories into a systematic mythology of Yapese culture, the people despaired because I had failed to comprehend that each was a distinctive, separate whole—meaningless out of context. I was approaching their cultural history in a segmented way. I sought to create a unified system, to sort all the pieces and to combine them into a systematic whole. The Yapese, on the other hand, were concerned about the integrity of each story and the social and political lessons and arguments that it contained. The parts of one story could not be added to the parts of another. Each story was complete in itself.

Dichotomistic versus Holistic Thinking

Marvin Mayers identifies two distinct orientations in thinking patterns: dichotomistic and holistic. Dichotomistic thinking is a pattern of segmental thinking in which people exhibit great concern for the particulars of a problem or situation and tend to reduce them to right and wrong options. A person with this type of thinking examines and sorts the details then reasons on the basis of perceived ordered relationships among them. Examples of such thinking include phonetic reading techniques in which words are broken into their syllables, pastimes such as Scrabble and crossword puzzles, and study techniques such as biblical word studies, sentence diagramming, and outlining. Holistic thinking is a pattern of thinking in which particulars are not separated from the context of the larger picture. A holistic thinker insists that the whole is greater than the parts and reasons on the basis of perceived relationships within the whole. Examples of such thinking include global look-and-say reading techniques in which words are learned as whole units, games such as checkers and chess, and study techniques such as memorization, imitation, and learning by participation (e.g., as an apprentice).

In American culture, one finds both dichotomistic and holistic patterns of thinking, and both affect the way people make judgments. Some Americans are reluctant to make a judgment about someone based on a specific behavior, preferring instead to evaluate a person's total behavior. Others, in contrast, make a judgment based on a specific behavior. We tend to evaluate others according to our predominant mode of thinking, a point illustrated by the following incident. An executive in a well-known evangelical school was caught in his office with his secretary sitting on his lap. For some members of his constituency, that act destroyed his ministry and tainted everything he had ever done—he was an immoral person, he was worthless, and his career was finished. These people reacted from what we would call a dichotomistic value orientation. The issues were black and white, and this man was judged on the basis of that single incident. The holistic thinkers who knew about the incident saw things differently. They evaluated this man not on the basis of that one act but on the basis of his entire career. Further, they pointed out that all are sinners and that each of us falls at one time or another. They asked, "Has he repented of his sin?" When they saw that he had repented, they recommended him for a different job in another Christian organization. From the perspective of the holist, this man's failure at one particular point in his life did not destroy a life of ministry in Christian service.

Table 3

Dichotomistic and Holistic Thinking

Dichotomistic Thinking	Holistic Thinking
1. Judgments are black/white, right/wrong—specific criteria are uniformly applied in evaluating others	1. Judgments are open-ended—the whole person and all circumstances are taken into consideration
2. Security comes from the feeling that one is right and fits into a particular role or category in society	2. Security comes from multiple interactions within the whole of society—one is insecure if confined to particular roles or categories
3. Information and experiences are systematically organized; details are sorted and ordered to form a clear pattern	3. Information and experiences are seemingly disorganized; details (narratives, events, portraits) stand as independent points complete in themselves

Dichotomistic thinkers tend to categorize people into specific roles. Once a person is labeled, the label defines his or her character and place, even though the label may not be a valid assessment of the person. People might be labeled good just because others do not know the faults or negative things in their lives. Holistic thinkers, in contrast, tend to withhold both approval and disapproval. They are somewhat suspicious of people who appear faultless and are more tentative about condemning the faulty.

The Yapese are quite holistic in their evaluation of others. In a series of extensive interviews with nearly one hundred men and fifty women, I asked each to name one person on Yap whom he or she admired. The most frequent response was "no one." As an American I was puzzled, and so I asked for an explanation of this response. The typical explanation was that everybody, without exception, had done something bad. If someone praised the governor for what he had accomplished, someone else would say, "Yes, but you know what he did to his wife!" or, "What about that incident when he was young? You see, he's no better than the rest of us."

Both holistic thinkers and dichotomistic thinkers may make negative value judgments about others but for different reasons. The dichotomist may reject a person because of a particular mistake, while a holist may say that all people are flawed because of any number of mistakes. Both may use their value orientation to reject others. The key moral issue here is not the way of thinking but what we do with the way we think. The Christian who rejects and maligns a fellow worker because of personal flaws or sins, whether thinking dichotomistically or holistically, is taking the matter of judgment into his or her own hands. Such a critical and judgmental attitude is a divisive and destructive force in any community.

Dual-Brain Theory

The differences between dichotomistic and holistic ways of thinking may originate in the distribution of thought processes in the human brain. The brain has two distinctive hemispheres. Numerous studies have been conducted regarding the different functions of the two hemispheres, and much more research is in progress. While the human brain is exceedingly complex, and some early research has been rejected as an oversimplification of the complexities, certain functions do seem to be located predominantly in one hemisphere or the other. Rita Carter (1998) suggests that thought processes are distributed as follows:

Table 4

Left Hemisphere	Right Hemisphere
analytical	holistic
logical	emotional
precise	pattern recognition
time sensitive	sensory

The two hemispheres are connected by tissue known as the corpus callosum, which functions as the communication link between them. In treating epileptic patients, doctors have sometimes severed the corpus callosum. The result is a "split brain" incapable of communicating across the hemispheres. Studies of such patients have produced provocative insights into the different functions of each brain hemisphere. For example, a split-brain patient was asked to feel an object with his left hand and to identify it. The patient expressed familiarity with the object but was unable to name it. However, when he held the object in his right hand, he had no trouble identifying it.

For most people the center of verbal expression is in the left brain, which is also the nerve center for the right hand. When the object was in the patient's left hand, the speech center in his left brain had no information with which to generate speech. The right brain registered the form of the object as familiar, but without the corpus callosum, it could not transmit that image to the left hemisphere, where verbal association could be made.

Both hemispheres are essential for a healthy life (a split brain is a malfunctioning brain), and one might argue that both kinds of thinking are advantageous for any individual and culture. Research on the brain function of famous musicians has demonstrated that creativity requires use of both hemispheres of the brain and complex exchange of information between them. Artists who have suffered partial brain damage through a stroke or other injury have lost their creative abilities, even though part of their musical skill has remained intact. Each healthy individual uses both hemispheres of the brain, but generally one side tends to dominate the other. At a simple level, people differ by thinking predominantly either in mental images or in words. Individuals with a dominant left hemisphere may often think largely in the verbal or language mode, whereas individuals with a dominant right hemisphere may often think largely in concrete images or the sensory mode. When one type of thinking completely suppresses the other, the individual may suffer a loss of functional capacities.

An incident of storytelling illustrates right-hemisphere dominance and the interplay between hemispheres. Shortly after arriving in the United States for schooling, a Yapese teenager told me in Yapese a long, detailed legend about a freshwater well on the tidal flats near her home. Three years later she related the same story to me again, but this time in English. As she told the story the second time, she occasionally struggled to find the appropriate English words. I suggested she use Yapese, but she could not remember the Yapese words since she had not heard or used them for three years. She said she pictured the story in her mind and then searched for the words to describe the places and action visible in her memory. Her first language, Yapese, had faded from her left-brain memory, but the pictorial images of the story were still vivid in her right brain.

Thinking Patterns in Particular Cultures

Many anthropologists view culture as a collective product created by individual minds. With this understanding of culture we might, as we compare the differences between western and non-western (e.g., Hebrew) cultures, say that the development of culture in the West has been largely influenced by people whose thinking has been analytical and dichotomistic, while Hebrew and other non-western cultures have been largely influenced by people whose thinking has been synthetic and holistic.

Anthropologist Thomas Gladwin (1970) contrasts westerners' solutions for navigational problems with those of the Puluwat (of Micronesia). The Puluwat navigators employ visual sightings of stars, the sun, and birds and listen to the varying sounds of waves on the hulls of their canoes to set their course, but they cannot verbalize the solution arrived at or the reasoning used to reach it. Western navigators, in contrast, use a magnetic compass and a sextant to determine an abstract location and a course of direction on a grid of the earth, and they can freely verbalize the logic and rationale behind actions taken. Anthony Paredes and Marcus Hepburn (1976) argue that the Puluwatese employ right-hemisphere thinking and the western navigators use left-hemisphere thinking, which they have learned from their respective predecessors.

A similar explanation might be given for the difference between prophetic writings in the Old Testament and in the Pauline Epistles. Isaiah, Jeremiah, Ezekiel, and the Minor Prophets describe specific historical incidents or concrete pictographic visions in great detail for their readers. Paul, in contrast, argues in abstract, often difficult logic (e.g., Romans 4–5) to convince his readers of his point. Paul uses the verbal, abstract, and rational thinking that was characteristic of Greek philosophy rather than the pictorial, concrete, and emotional thinking that was characteristic of the Hebrew prophets.

The tradition of systematic theology grew out of the Greek philosophical perspective, which was analytical, as opposed to the holistic orientation evident in the Hebrew texts. John Levinson (1999) details the way in which Greco-Roman thought stimulated a significant shift in Jewish views and writing. The inspiration of Scripture, seen as an ecstatic, noncognitive process by Old Testament writers, was viewed as an engaged, cognitive process by Josephus and Jewish writers of the New Testament period. The analytical methodology of systematic theology employs mechanisms of sorting, comparison, and contrast, which theologians use to take apart texts and put them into constructed systems of theological thought. Some contemporary scholars have reacted to the traditional analytical methods and the distortions to the biblical text that sometimes result. First biblical theologians (Conn 1984) and then narrative theologians (Loughlin 1996; Cook 1997) sought to conduct theology using more holistic methods, treating texts as complete narratives that must be considered in their own right. Those conducting narrative theology took a further step, arguing that the church is comprised of distinctive cultural communities, and each community must engage the narratives and interpret them in light of its own contemporary cultural context.

Although hemispheric dominance limits the creativity of individuals and cultures, the general tendency is toward extremes. Western analytic schooling and religious denominations suppress the concrete, emotional, and synthetic thinkers, while non-western cultures such as Yap, Truk, and traditional African suppress their analytic and abstract thinkers. This may be one factor in the rapid spread of Pentecostal Christianity in Latin America at the expense of Catholics and Protestant evangelicals, who are rational and analytic in their approaches.

The Model of Jesus

The challenge facing those in missions and ministry is to learn to think in accordance with the mind-set and culture of those with whom they work. Once again the life and work of Christ provide the example for us. We have already observed that Jesus grew up in the culture of his day and participated in all the learning and living activities common to the people around him. He was so ordinary in this regard that people in his hometown refused to accept the power of his teaching and ministry (Matt. 13:54–58).

Jesus mastered the content of Jewish life and culture. He understood clearly the contemporary social structure, with its distinctions between rich and poor, its political and religious parties, and the hierarchy of leadership within these groups. He had a thorough grasp of the religious traditions and of the way the leaders abused those traditions for personal prestige and economic gain. He knew the Scriptures better than they did, not because he had magical insight but because, as he studied and learned the Scriptures, his understanding was not clouded by personal sin.

Jesus not only grasped the content of Jewish life and culture but also discerned the workings of the minds of the people. None of the twelve disciples whom he chose was of the educated elite. Only Paul, an apostle after Jesus' death and resurrection, came from that stratum of society. The twelve were commoners and, to the best of our knowledge, were trained only in the workplace of their occupations. From the evidence presented in their writings, the disciples were generally what we have described as holistic thinkers.

The evidence is circumstantial, but the Gospel writings suggest that as Jesus taught he utilized right-hemisphere, pictorial, concrete, holistic, and analogic strategies rather than left-hemisphere, verbal, abstract, dichotomistic, and analytic thought. One of the techniques used throughout Matthew, for example, is that of concrete analogy. Matthew 5:13–14 compares the believer to salt and light. Salt without flavor and a light under a basket are worthless. In Matthew 16, Jesus uses the metaphor of yeast in regard to the teachings of the Pharisees. The Gospel of John reports that Jesus spoke of himself as the Good Shepherd, the living water, the bread of life, and the vine—all significant analogies that communicated the truth about himself. The objects that Jesus chose as analogies were common, everyday aspects of Jewish culture, familiar to everyone who heard his message.

The parables are a more complex form of analogy. Jesus created stories to illustrate and teach particular truths. Each story portrayed incidents from the ordinary cultural life of the people of his day such as sowing seed, removing weeds from the wheat, paying laborers in a vineyard, and attending a wedding. If the point of the story was not obvious to the hearers and to his disciples, Jesus explained more specifically its meaning.

Another technique Jesus used involved focusing on issues of his day to teach spiritual truth. In Matthew 9, he uses the issue of fasting to emphasize that his teaching cannot be poured into traditional Jewish cultural containers. In Matthew 12, he raises the issues of plucking grain and healing on the Sabbath to teach God's priority of mercy and his own lordship of the Sabbath. Time and again he addresses the social injustices of contemporary life. In the Sermon on the Mount, by focusing on internal motives rather than external acts, he attacks the legalistic application of the law; he levels the charge that anger is murder and lust is adultery and insists that truth replace oath taking and mercy replace the principle of an eye for an eye. He addresses taxes, marriage, divorce, prayer, care of the elderly, and the struggles for political and economic power at the expense of "the more important matters of the law—justice, mercy and faithfulness" (Matt. 23:23). In addressing each of these issues, Jesus uses powerful concrete illustrations and verbal images to drive home his point: "You blind guides! You strain out a gnat but swallow a camel" (v. 24); "You clean the outside of the cup and dish, but inside they are full of greed and self-indulgence" (v. 25).

The other predominant method of teaching employed by Jesus is the personal object lesson. In Matthew 8–9, a series of case studies portrays Jesus' healing ministry. In the story of the leper, Jesus touches and heals a man labeled by society as untouchable. In the story of the centurion and his servant, Jesus marvels at the centurion's faith and with a spoken word heals a man who is not physically present. With a touch Jesus heals Peter's mother-in-law, and he forgives the sins of a paralyzed man before he commands the man to take up his mat and go home. In each of these incidents, we see in concrete actions the deity, humanity, and personal work of Christ.

The impact of the Gospel narratives is concrete and holistic. Jesus drives home his message with one powerful image after another, using illustrations from nature, tradition, and daily life. The learner is challenged to think with geometric intuition rather than algebraic analysis. Jesus asks questions and refuses to give the answers. He refutes the accepted knowledge of his day (e.g., Matt. 22:41–46) and confronts his hearers with penetrating insight as to how the Scriptures apply to their daily lives.

Charles Kraft (1983, 28) succinctly summarizes Jesus' approach as "receptor-oriented and personal," a model that should be our goal as we attempt to communicate in Christian ministry. If Jesus were to go to Yap, he would learn to think as the Yapese think. He would listen to their conversations, observe their society and culture at work, and internalize their world-and-life view. Then he would communicate and teach as the Yapese teach, using parables and case studies to illustrate particular truths, sitting with them in discussion, asking them questions, debating the answers, and drawing from their experience, traditions, and beliefs the illustrations and analogies that would open their eyes to God's truth and would challenge their unbelief and resistance to him.

Implications for Cross-Cultural Ministry

We have considered at some length how people differ in their brain function. Some demonstrate segmental-thinking styles in which the left brain dominates; others demonstrate holistic-thinking styles in which the right brain dominates. Further, we find that these differences in thought patterns produce significantly different and often opposing value orientations. Segmental thinkers demand clear-cut, black-and-white answers, insist on the universal application of principles, and cannot feel secure unless their perceptions are recognized as correct. This particular pattern of thought was typical of the Jewish leaders who challenged Jesus repeatedly during his ministry (e.g., Luke 20:1–8). It was also typical of the many missionaries who challenged Hudson Taylor's innovative life-style and ministry in China during the last century.

Holistic thinkers, on the other hand, see most issues as gray (open for debate) rather than black and white. They believe that each situation is unique and are uncomfortable with standardized procedures and rigidly applied rules. They resist being pinned down to a particular position on an issue or to a particular social role. This pattern of thinking character-ized Jesus' treatment of those religious leaders who insisted on rigid adherence to traditional Jewish law. For example, in Luke 20, when Jewish leaders questioned the source of Jesus' authority, he broadened the question to include the authority of John and the character of the questioners (vv. 3–4, 9–19). He forced them to consider other related issues by overturning their traditions (such as buying and selling in the temple) and quoting Scripture to show their hypocrisy (Luke 19:45–46). Hudson Taylor made similar demands on his missionary col-leagues, forcing them to consider Chinese expectations and showing them how their acceptance of Chinese ways opened the Chinese people to the gospel.

A missionary entering another culture must realize that people evaluate others in different ways. Islamic people will judge an outsider according to the rigid, dichotomistic stan-dards of Islam and according to the outsider's specific role among them. The Yapese will evaluate someone from another culture not on the basis of role but on the basis of the total person. They will watch all the activities and interactions of the newcomer. No matter how good a job one does, the Yapese will be quick to play up faults and weaknesses.

The Yapese pattern contrasts sharply with that of American culture and society. Americans evaluate others primarily on the basis of their role performance. Teachers are considered good or bad not on the basis of how they treat their families but on the basis of how they perform for the brief time in the classroom. In America, we find out very little about others as persons because we do not take the time or have the opportunity to observe them. We do not see how others treat their children or spouse, what they do when they get up in the morning, or how they behave in private. We see each person as playing a specific role. Dichotomistic thinkers probably like or dislike someone on the basis of the specifics of his or her performance, while holistic thinkers withhold judgment until they feel they know the person.

The way we think predisposes how we will judge others. Dichotomistic thinkers will reject the muddy ambiguity of their holist peers, accusing them of softness, lack of principle, and inconsistency. Holistic thinkers will reject the rigidity of their dichotomist peers, accusing them of legalism and callous inhumanity toward others. Such personal rejections, however, come only from limited perspectives. This is why Christ warns in Matthew 7:1, "Do not judge, or you too will be judged," and Paul says, "I do not even judge myself" (1 Cor. 4:3). Jesus, in contrast, knows our hearts, and he alone, Paul tells us, will be the judge of men (Rom. 2:16; 1 Cor. 4:4–5) and of the effectiveness of a particular ministry.

One of the biggest problems in our families, churches, and missions is that we often insist that others think and judge in the same way we do. We do not accept one another in love; rather, we try to remake those around us into our own image. This tendency is the negation of the principle of incarnation, which requires that we learn to think in the style of our neighbor. We must remember that a split brain is a malfunctioning brain, that each part of the body is important to God, and that the unity of the whole is pleasing to him (Psalm 133; 1 Cor. 12:12–13).

___ | five ___

Tensions Associated
with Handling Crises

One Saturday morning on Yap in 1979, I was reading and listening to background music on the radio when the announcer interrupted the program to say that early that morning there had been a typhoon in the Woleai area, several hundred miles east of Yap. The storm was moving toward Yap and was expected to arrive sometime Monday morning. Remembering the typhoon we had experienced there twelve years earlier, I set the book aside to find my wife and give her the news. A half hour later the radio announcer repeated the warning, spurring me to go through the village and warn some Yapese friends who were working at a sawmill they had built on the beach. Because two of these men had jobs in town during the week, they worked hard on Saturday cutting lumber. When I informed them about the typhoon and its expected arrival on Monday, they reacted by saying, "No problem! We'll get ready for the typhoon tomorrow." They continued working, and I returned home.

After lunch I tuned in again to hear the announcer report that weather-tracking stations had found that the typhoon was moving faster than anticipated and would reach Yap sometime Sunday afternoon. My anxiety increased somewhat, and I went to my neighbor and asked if he had heard about the coming typhoon. "Ah," he said, "there's no typhoon coming. You can't believe what you hear on the radio. Don't worry about it. When there's a typhoon, I'll let you know!" So I returned home while my friends and my neighbor continued their activities. I had less peace of mind than they, however, so I sat down on the porch where I could watch the surf, remembering that during the last typhoon the waves at high tide had breached the crest of the beach, flooding the land on which our houses were built. Ordinarily, high tides lap close to the crest but never go over.

About half past four that afternoon, as I sat on the porch and watched, a wave washed gently over the crest. Without hesitation I ran into the house and told my wife to grab what she needed—the typhoon was here! I jumped into the car to move it to high ground. I had not gone a quarter of a mile before the sea surged inland and I was driving through salt water. After driving the car to safety on higher ground behind a friend's house, I rushed to the beach. There I found my friends working frantically in waist-deep water to remove the sawmill engine from its mounts. By the time we got the engine to a pickup truck, the waves were pounding us, and water flooded the motor of the truck. Miraculously, the truck started, and we managed to move it to the high ground behind the house. Meanwhile, the sawed lumber floated in every direction. My neighbor, who had said he would let me know when there was a typhoon, never had the opportunity. He, like everyone else, was working frantically to salvage what he could from the water.

After the storm, I remembered that on Friday evening, when I had passed the Coast Guard's Loran Station high on the plateau, all of its windows had been battened down with plywood. The Yapese and I had ignored this, since we had as yet heard nothing about a storm. The Coast Guard, however, monitored long-term weather forecasts in the area and even before the news broke on the radio had received the early warnings and had taken all the necessary precautions. While we were struggling frantically in the wind and water, the men at the Coast Guard station were watching a movie secure in their concrete buildings in the highlands.

Crisis Orientation versus Noncrisis Orientation

The typhoon incident illustrates two different attitudes toward potential crises. The Coast Guard strategy exemplifies what Marvin Mayers calls a crisis orientation, and the Yapese strategy represents a noncrisis orientation. The mission of the Coast Guard is to look for potential problems and to solve them before they happen or to bring existing crises to a swift resolution. The Coast Guard has a manual of procedures that specifies the decision to be made in various situations. The manual is authoritative and limits the officers to specified steps they should follow for each type of crisis discussed. An officer who fails to follow the manual is reprimanded. Because of their crisis orientation, the men at the Coast Guard station were free to relax and wait out the typhoon in the security of their quarters.

The Yapese are familiar with precautionary procedures, since the district government has a similar manual regarding typhoons. Most Yapese, however, have a noncrisis orientation, and so they ignore these procedures. Like my neighbors who told me not to worry and continued their activities, most Yapese downplay the likelihood of a crisis and avoid taking action on an issue as long as possible. When a crisis is imminent, they derive their solutions from whatever alternatives they perceive in the situation. Whether to save the pickup truck and/or the sawmill engine or to chance losing both is a decision they make during the storm as they struggle against the wind, waves, and other dangers. All of this is not without a measure of humor; while we were carrying the sawmill engine, we stopped and laughed at the sight of a house floating down the road.

While the Coast Guard's strategies seem more practical to the American mind, the Yapese also have sound reasons for their behavior. Although two or three storms have been known to strike the island in a single year, the last typhoon they had experienced was in 1967, twelve years earlier. Yet each year Yap receives warnings of at least twenty typhoons. Since these storms are so unpredictable, the Yapese are skeptical of weather bureau warnings and refuse to expend the effort necessary to clear everything from the shoreline and to get their homes and boathouses ready to withstand a possible storm. Their attitude is to wait until the typhoon is a reality, then do what they must to cope. Sometimes they are caught completely unprepared, and then it takes them about five days to clean up. However, if one considers the amount of labor saved by not responding to the warnings regarding the storms that ultimately veer away, over the long term the Yapese come out ahead. They may lose a few things in the process, but they are willing to accept that cost.

The Yapese extend this noncrisis orientation to many areas of life and typically ignore potential problems until they happen. For example, when a child is having difficulty in school, many parents do not admonish the child or inquire at the school until something happens to precipitate a crisis. The complex reasons for this are rooted in Yapese ideals regarding parent-child relationships. The Yapese community stresses that parents are directly responsible for the behavior of their children. In return for parental nurture, children are expected to give unquestioning obedience and respect. As a consequence, many children feel a sense of shame and failure when they cause trouble or do poorly in school. When parents become aware of a child's problems, they are afraid to get involved, believing that the child might feel such great shame that he or she will stop going to school altogether or will run away. Some children have even attempted suicide when their shame was excessive. Fearing such dire consequences associated with becoming involved, the Yapese try to downplay personal crises and wait for problems to work themselves out.

Two Styles of Crisis Management

The procedures for managing actual crises also differ. Those with a crisis orientation emphasize precise authoritative procedures geared to a specific situation. For example, Coast Guard officers follow an operations manual that spells out the correct procedures for most of the situations for which they may someday be responsible. Officers follow those procedures exactly and expect them to work. Although personnel changes year after year, Coast Guard operations and crisis management remain consistently the same. This pattern of crisis management is characteristic of the entire American military system. A navy friend of mine, Jim, was in charge of the nuclear firing devices on a particular vessel and was responsible for the security of the area. In practice drills, his commanding officer would frequently violate this forbidden area to test Jim's ability to respond to crisis. Each time Jim managed to "kill" his commanding officer, his performance was rated satisfactory. If he failed, he received a demerit. One night a couple of drunken sailors from another ship overcame a guard, took his gun, and entered the prohibited area. The alarm sounded, and in less than two minutes, Jim was out of his bunk and had subdued and disarmed the men. He had practiced this procedure so many times that it had become automatic. Repetitious drill had effectively prepared him for the real crisis when it happened. This type of crisis management reflects an extreme crisis orientation. The Yapese would never dream of introducing that kind of procedure into their culture, although they can learn it, just as we can and do.

The noncrisis orientation is experience-focused; when a crisis arises, those with this orientation choose from among multiple options for resolving the problem. The way the Yapese respond to typhoons serves as an illustration. From their experience, the Yapese know that far more warnings than actual storms come to Yap. Further, when a storm does come, its direction determines its major effects. If a storm brings high water, the Yapese rescue items such as the sawmill engine. If, on the other hand, the wind is severe, they endeavor to secure objects that may blow away or injure others. They tackle the problems unique to each storm, protecting material possessions most immediately affected. For example, in 1967, my new house was saved because a few men worked in the water during the storm, shoving logs away from the house before the waves could turn them into battering rams.

Declarative versus Interrogative Lifestyle

Individuals as well as cultures differ in their orientation toward and management of crisis. Those with a noncrisis orientation tend to take things as they come; they do not expect or look for problems. Those who are crisis-oriented, however, tend to examine every activity for potential flaws or problems. The noncrisis-oriented person tends to be optimistic; the crisis-oriented person pessimistic.

Crisis-oriented persons embrace what Mayers has termed a declarative lifestyle. In their view, crises should be avoided when at all possible, and careful planning is done to anticipate problems. Declarative persons seek out expert advice and are single-minded in applying that advice when they face crises. When a crisis does arise, they work rapidly to resolve the issue. Further, once they have identified an efficient procedure, they use it repeatedly rather than try something new or different.

Noncrisis-oriented persons follow what Mayers has termed an interrogative lifestyle. Their brand of crisis management is experience-oriented, and they choose from multiple procedures and options. Such persons decide between alternatives that emerge from each new situation, and their style of management is open-ended. They can tolerate considerable ambiguity in their lives and do not push for an early resolution of conflict. Further, seeing themselves as qualified by their own experiences to manage each situation, they are skeptical of experts.

Table 5

Crisis and Noncrisis Orientations

Crisis Orientation	Noncrisis Orientation
1. Anticipates crisis	1. Downplays possibility of crisis
2. Emphasizes planning	2. Focuses on actual experience
3. Seeks quick resolution to avoid ambiguity	3. Avoids taking action; delays decisions
4. Repeatedly follows a single authoritative, preplanned procedure	4. Seeks ad hoc solutions from multiple available options
5. Seeks expert advice	5. Distrusts expert advice

Crisis Management and Cross-Cultural Ministry

Mission and church organizations attract both types of people. Noncrisis-oriented administrators have an abundance of new ideas and interests as well as an optimism that everything can be done with the present staff and resources. They ignore both potential and real problems and often refuse to seek advice from experts. The crisis-oriented persons on their staff shake their heads in dismay at the lack of planning and predictability. Crises arise with startling frequency, and the crisis-oriented individual rebels at the lack of preparation and the unpredictability of the situation. Individuals in conflict begin to question the spiritual commitment of one another as the stress of the situation takes its toll on their emotional and physical well-being. Some individuals leave the organization because the style of management produces more stress than they can endure.

Crisis-oriented administrators have a different problem. For them, plans and procedures supersede the needs of the people concerned. The workings of the organization are tightly regulated, and growth and change are planned years in advance. When a problem occurs, the contingency plan is implemented quickly, with expert direction, to bring resolution as soon as possible. Individuals who are not capable of working within the plan or who are out of step with it are bypassed, overruled, or even dismissed from the organization.

When national church leaders and foreign missionaries attempt to work together, these differences may be further exacerbated, for cultural conflicts add to the problems caused by differences in management style. This tension is illustrated by the following incident.

The 1979 typhoon on Yap did some damage to the youth center of the Yap Evangelical Church, peeling up a section of the roof and exposing an area used as a classroom for children. The mission teacher was very much concerned because her school materials were located in this area, and, if it were to rain, they could be damaged. So she told the Yapese pastor that this was an urgent matter. The pastor agreed and said that he would send word to Andrew, who was in charge of maintenance, to repair the roof. The teacher waited for a couple days, but Andrew did not appear. She began to be very anxious, thinking that it might rain at any time. Further, she did not want to conduct school until the roof was fixed. She discussed the matter with some other missionaries, and they decided to contact a Filipino construction group. Men from this group came the next day and quickly made the repairs.

Shortly thereafter Andrew heard about the Filipinos' work and was deeply hurt. From his point of view the matter had not been urgent; after a typhoon there is usually a period of a couple weeks without rain. His house had suffered considerable damage in the storm, whereas the roof of the youth center had sustained only minor damage. Since it had not rained, no further damage had been done. He complained to the Yapese pastor, "I have built every building in this place. I've made every repair that has ever been needed, and I would have made this one. Why didn't they wait for me and trust me?"

The conflict between missionary and national arose because of their different orientations with regard to crisis. If it had started to rain, Andrew would have dropped whatever he was doing and would have gone to town immediately to repair the roof. But each morning he studied the sky and, after concluding that there would be no rain that day, continued to work on his house. To him, until it started to rain, there was no crisis; besides, in just a couple days, he would have been ready to work on the roof anyway. But the teacher, compelled by a crisis orientation and a need for resolution, could not tolerate her uncertainty about his coming and her anxiety about potential disaster.

For crisis-oriented missionaries and other outsiders, the noncrisis orientation produces not only frustration and anxiety but also serious breakdown in communication and mutual support. Another example from Yap illustrates this problem. An American pilot working with Pacific Missionary Aviation on Yap was flying in a patient from the island of Ulithi. The patient was hemorrhaging badly, so the pilot radioed to the hospital requesting an ambulance. The ambulance attendants were noncrisis-oriented Yapese who seldom got calls for an ambulance and hardly ever experienced a genuine crisis. When the pilot landed at the airport, there was no ambulance, and the patient died in the airplane. When the ambulance finally arrived about a half hour later, the pilot was livid and threatened to maim the driver. A Yapese mechanic, seeing the pilot's anger, ran to the driver and said, "He's so mad at you that he's going to kill you; you'd better get out of here!" At that point the driver fled back to town in the ambulance, leaving the pilot to take the body to the hospital.

If we are involved in Christian ministry, we must expect that our sense of urgency may not be shared by others. We must ask ourselves, Is the problem as critical as we believe it to be? How much damage will really occur if the job is not done? What options are open to us should the expected crisis occur? In the case of the teacher, a simple way to alleviate anxiety would have been to move her classroom materials, because much of the roof had not been damaged. In the case of the pilot, however, the very real crisis ended with the death of his patient.

In regard to the pilot's case, it is easy simply to criticize the ambulance attendants and to exonerate the pilot. The pilot, however, had failed to establish a relationship with the attendants prior to the incident. He had failed to communicate with them, and thus they did not know what kinds of radio messages he might send to them during flight. He had not prepared to handle a critical situation within a noncrisis-oriented culture. The message he conveyed during the crisis seemed urgent to him but not to those who received it. He assumed the Yapese would understand him and respond as he (and people from his own culture) would respond. When they did not, he became enraged at them for not understanding him, although he had never made a serious effort to understand them or their particular orientation with regard to crisis.

A common error in cross-cultural ministry is assuming that people understand us when they hear our words. We fail to see that differing personal orientations can prevent mutual understanding. Further, we assume that our style of decision making and crisis management is the best one. We must ask whether it is more important to do it our way or to work together with the people around us, building mutual understanding and cooperating to make decisions and solve crises in a manner acceptable and beneficial to the entire community. Crisis-oriented and noncrisis-oriented persons have much to contribute to one another, but this can be accomplished only when there is an attitude of mutual understanding and acceptance.

The Biblical Perspective

Many missionaries, pastors, and lay workers tend to judge issues only in spiritual terms and fail to see the cultural dimension. They can readily cite Scripture to support their own viewpoint as to how things ought to be done. However, they may be blind to scriptural evidence that another way might also have biblical precedent and support. When we examine the life of Christ, for example, we find that Jesus often demonstrated a noncrisis orientation. The Jewish leadership, on the other hand, had a crisis orientation to issues of the day. The law and traditions were their authoritative guide, and, pointing to this guide, they sought to coerce Jesus to resolve issues quickly. But Jesus responded with questions rather than with answers (e.g., Luke 20:3) and with parables that raised issues rather than brought resolution. Moreover, he slept in a boat during a storm, taught and healed until it was so late that people had to be fed, delayed en route to the respective homes of Jairus and Lazarus (so that in both cases the ill person died), and walked calmly into the hands of his betrayer.

The implication is that although Jesus demands a firm decision when we commit ourselves to him, we must be open-minded in our ensuing service. In Luke 9:23, he warns, "If anyone would come after me, he must deny himself and take up his cross daily and follow me." According to this statement, there is no room for wavering or for delay. Yet in the very next chapter (Luke 10:1–12), he instructs those he is sending out to accept whatever circumstances arise as they follow him. He commands them to make no advance preparation but to stay wherever they are welcomed, eat whatever they are given, minister to those in need, and teach those who will listen.

For the Christian laborer, then, the challenge is to have an unwavering declarative commitment to the gospel and an open, questioning, noncrisis-oriented lifestyle and ministry. Paul charges Timothy, "Be prepared in season and out of season; correct, rebuke and encourage—with great patience and careful instruction" (2 Tim. 4:2). The command to be prepared suggests that a crisis orientation is needed so that the servant is ready for preaching and teaching opportunities, whereas the instruction to serve "with great patience" suggests a noncrisis orientation in personal life and ministry to others.

As Christian workers, we cannot escape Paul's challenge that we are to be like Christ, taking the very nature of a servant (Phil. 2:5–7). Such servanthood requires that we become all things to the people we serve (1 Cor. 9:19–23). If some people think in ways different from ours, we must learn to think as they think. If some people respond to crises and make decisions in ways different from ours, we must learn their crisis-management style. Our goal must be to build up the unity and fellowship of the body of Christ. To achieve that goal, we must always consider others better than ourselves. Our role is to be that of a servant.

six

Tensions over Goals

A Yapese man in my village asked several of his friends and relatives to help him do some work. He set the date and requested that they come at ten in the morning. Understanding how Yapese view time, I went at eleven to see what was happening, and as I expected, I found a few men sitting around and talking. By noon some other men had trickled in, and we continued to talk. At about three in the afternoon, one man excused himself, saying he had other obligations, and soon another had to leave. At that point one man joked that they had come to work but had not done a thing. They all laughed and then decided that they would not bother to begin working that day but would come back the following Thursday. Gradually they dispersed, having spent most of the day in conversation.

The next Thursday they gathered again, some men coming as early as nine o'clock and others around ten. By half past ten there were enough to begin working, so they worked a little while and then stopped to talk and chew betel nut. A couple of other men appeared; they worked for nearly an hour and then sat down to talk and chew betel nut. This routine was followed all day. By late afternoon the men had worked the equivalent of four hours and were satisfied that they had accomplished a good day's labor. As they left they agreed to work again in a couple of weeks.

An American might react to this work pattern with the comment, "No wonder things take years to get done!" But those Yapese men were quite happy with both of those days. Their goal, their objective, was not so much to complete the task as to enjoy the interaction, their coming together and talking to one another. On the first day they enjoyed their socializing so much that they ignored the task. On the second day the organizer did want to make progress on his project, but interaction was still an important part of their activity.

People from other cultures who have worked on Yap generally have not adopted Yapese work patterns—indeed, these workers have often found them incomprehensible. Korean and Japanese men employed there, for example, were renowned as hard workers and greatly impressed the Yapese with how much they could accomplish in a day as they repaired cars or labored in other jobs. However, these immigrants were paid on the basis of the quantity of work they completed; they were dependent on wages for their livelihood. Their economic needs often forced them to make the completion of their tasks their highest priority. The economic needs of the Yapese, in contrast, were met by subsistence agriculture. Group cooperation, which involved enjoying and building relationships with others, was as important to the maintenance of agriculture as was individual effort. As a consequence, the primary goal of the Yapese was not task completion but rather interaction with other people for mutually beneficial ends.

Task Orientation versus Person Orientation

Individuals who are task-oriented find satisfaction in reaching their objectives and completing their projects. Their lives are motivated and directed by an unending succession of objectives. Frequently they aspire to complete a greater number of tasks than is humanly possible in the time they allocate; as a result, their lives take on a frenetic pace filled with activities. Many become workaholics, allowing tasks to so dominate their lives that other people are viewed as merely a part of their work schedule.

The social life of task-oriented individuals is often merely an extension of work activity. At social gatherings their conversation is limited primarily to problems or concerns associated with their work. Other subjects (except for those that focus on another of their objectives) bore them. Task-oriented people consider social activities a drain on their productive time and often prefer the solitude of working alone and uninterrupted. To achieve is more important than to build social relationships, and they are willing to endure social deprivation to reach their goals.

Individuals who are person-oriented find their satisfaction in interaction with others. Their highest priority is to establish and maintain personal relationships, and they enjoy the social interaction required to sustain these relationships. Some take every available opportunity to meet new people and to culti-vate an extensive network of personal contacts.

People who have interaction as a goal need the accep-tance and stimulus of their group of associates. They must spend a significant amount of time and energy fulfilling the obligations of group membership and maintaining personal ties. They work hard to promote group interests and interaction, often sacrificing their own personal goals for the interests of others. Failure to accomplish a task is less critical to them than a gain in the quality of personal relationships.

Table 6

Task and Person Orientations

Task Orientation	Person Orientation
1. Focuses on tasks and principles	1. Focuses on persons and relationships
2. Finds satisfaction in the achievement of goals	2. Finds satisfaction in interaction
3. Seeks friends with similar goals	3. Seeks friends who are group-oriented
4. Accepts loneliness and social deprivation for the sake of personal achievements	4. Deplores loneliness; sacrifices personal achievements for group interaction

Task Orientation in Ministry

Missionaries, pastors, and lay workers who are task-oriented are well equipped for administrative responsibilities, for teaching, preaching, and Bible translation. As long as they are able to schedule their own activities and to work independently of others, they will be effective in their service. Their frustrations lie with their fellow workers. They are intolerant of others who show less commitment to the task at hand than they do, and they experience great aggravation with those who spend time in apparently frivolous conversation and whose lives are not organized around a list of objectives.

When task-oriented individuals serve as missionaries in a person-oriented culture, they often fail to grasp the importance of interaction in the daily work routine and become extremely judgmental of their national coworkers. For example, Americans in Micronesia may notice their national colleagues talking for long periods during the workday and may accuse them of being lazy and unproductive. These Americans, however, have failed to comprehend that social interaction is part of the Micronesian daily routine of working and has been so for hundreds of years. Further, they have failed to see the same pattern in the New Testament, even though it occurs there repeatedly. They have been blinded by their own cultural values.

Person Orientation in Ministry

Micronesians are not the only interaction-oriented people. Many Americans, in fact, have personal relationships as their central goal, and, conversely, many Micronesians focus primarily on tasks to be accomplished. In both cases, these individuals are pushing against the current of the values of their culture. American society views negatively the highly social but nonproductive person, while Micronesian societies disapprove of the individual who appears to be hard, unkind, and striving. For mission work, these differences suggest that the most productive Americans may not be the best people to send to interaction-oriented non-western cultures and that the most productive nationals may not be the best candidates for church leadership.

The western educational system is not designed to reward individuals who are person-oriented. These students often struggle to meet the schedules and demands of learning and are unwilling to sacrifice interpersonal ties for long hours of study. Their academic records may be poorer than those of their task-oriented peers. It should be evident by now, however, that performance in school is not always a reliable indicator of potential success in ministry.

Another problem is that success in ministry is difficult to define. Since task-oriented people with high academic credentials are often the leaders in church and mission organizations, success is often defined in terms of objective goals. The person-oriented members of their organizations often fall short of such goals yet may have excellent relationships and a strong personal ministry. Sometimes leaders exert great pressure on person-oriented coworkers to conform to the expected pattern and may even view them as having a spiritual problem of resisting authority.

It should be apparent that we need to offer more encouragement to those among us who by nature are person-oriented. They bring a special gift to ministry that others must struggle to learn. We also need to reassess the standards by which we select missionaries and nationals to be church leaders and by which we recognize them for service.

Conflict over Goals

When Micronesians get together to work, their social interaction is just as important to them as getting the job done. Unfortunately, many task-oriented missionaries fail to comprehend or accept such a value. As a consequence, they end up rejecting the very people to whom they feel called to minister. From their value perspective, work and interaction do not belong to the same process. Micronesians, on the other hand, believe that work without significant interaction is selfish and unsatisfying.

My own response to some Palauan men who constructed my house on Yap in 1967 is a good illustration of how a task-oriented person responds to the interaction-oriented Micronesian work pattern. A Palauan signed a contract calling for four men to construct my house at a cost of several hundred dollars. The contract specified that if the job took more than fifteen days, they would forfeit 10 percent for each day over the limit; if it took less than fifteen days, they would receive the full amount.

On the first day of work I went out to observe and found that instead of four men there were six. I thought, "Good. They will get the job done faster." But as I watched, they worked for an hour and then rested for an hour, a pattern they continued all day. By the end of the day I was really upset. I thought that they would never finish in fifteen days. I complained to the Filipino businessman who had arranged the contract. I wrote a letter to my uncle, a carpenter in California, expressing amazement at how the Palauans worked. Having spent only three weeks on Yap and never before having been exposed to another culture, I was astounded as these men sat and chewed betel nut and talked, working only roughly half of an eight-hour day. Yet unbelievably, six days later they finished the house.

I could not comprehend their strategy. Why did they bring two extra men? Why not use four men, work all day, and make more money? I later came to understand that for Micronesians a major incentive in doing a job is interaction. If they cannot enjoy themselves and talk to one another, there is little reason to work. Their goal is not to make all the money they can. Indeed, the six had other jobs, and the day they finished my house, they went back to their regular employment, where they made an hourly wage. They were concerned more with the interaction than with the pay.

Many western missionaries believe that we must dichotomize our work and our social interaction. In industrial societies, the coffee break, or interaction time, is clearly separated from the work time. Many missionaries have asked me, a self-confessed task-oriented person, how I could adjust to the change. My response is based on two principles. First, I accept the fact that I am what I am and that God wants me and will use me as I am. Second, I try to obey the admonition in Philippians 2:3: "Do nothing out of selfish ambition or vain conceit, but in humility consider others better than yourselves."

Some of my personal struggles will serve to illustrate how difficult it is to apply these principles. I went to Yap in 1967 to do research for a Ph.D. at the University of Pittsburgh. I knew that if I did not produce something substantial, I would not receive the degree. One does not get a doctorate just by sitting around and talking and chewing betel nut. I had to have something to show for my time in the field, and so I felt an invisible but ever present pressure. My work, like that of many missionaries, involved talking to people. I wanted to learn all I could about Yapese culture, so I always had questions to ask, and I took notes frequently. The questions and talking satisfied my concern for task completion. My work required interacting with people, but essentially I was collecting information.

This type of activity demanded an adjustment in my work habits, but I did not realize that it also required a change in how I evaluated other people. Sometimes I could not direct the conversation to topics I was interested in, and as a result, I soon became quite bored with the conversation. My lack of interest in the Yapese as people became apparent. I found it very difficult to interact with them when the conversation focused on things that I considered inane. At such times I wanted to get away from them and get on with my task, a desire that reflected my lack of commitment to persons.

This issue is important to any cross-cultural worker but is fundamental to the missionary. The missionary is sent to people to serve them, to minister to them, to communicate God's love for them. Building relationships is central to ministry. A missionary must devote his or her time and life to personal interaction. This means the task-oriented individual must consciously allocate significant amounts of time to sit and talk with people, for without a conscious effort, tasks will exhaust all available time and energy.

For the workaholic, casual conversation can be more difficult than a hundred chores. While such people may outwardly appear to be listening, inwardly they are thinking of all the things they could be doing instead. They find it extremely difficult to concentrate on people when there is so much to be done. Their body is present, but their mind is somewhere else, working on some other task. This is a critical problem for missionaries because people are sensitive and are often aware of this rejection.

It is important for task-oriented people to recognize that their striving after objective goals is a character flaw if the compulsion to work becomes obsessive. As Christians we want to reach people for Christ, but we often push people out of our activities. It does not matter how many buildings we build or how many reports we submit. If we are not meeting people and loving them through interaction, we have lost sight of the Great Commission and our activities have lost significance. We can sit at a desk and pour out our lives into a Bible translation or other Christian work, but the people out there in the world will never see that we love them. At a desk we rarely talk to them, we rarely interact with them, we seldom show them that we care. We do not go out and work at their side. It is important to realize that, although we might be doing a work of love with our hands or heart or mind, unless we show people our love in a personal way by interacting with them as individuals, our work will mean nothing to them.

The Biblical Perspective

"As apostles of Christ, we could have been a burden to you, but we were gentle among you, like a mother caring for her little children. We loved you so much that we were delighted to share with you not only the gospel of God but our lives as well, because you had become so dear to us" (1 Thess. 2:6–8). Paul's example is one that we should admire and look to as a guide for own lives and ministries. We know from his letters that he did not impose the strict discipline of the Jewish lifestyle on his Gentile converts. Further, he saw the necessity of sharing his life, not just the gospel message.

Each of us has different talents. Some have a gift for interacting with people. Others have a gift for achieving objective goals. All of us who aspire to Christian ministry and service must seek to increase our concern for and interaction with others, or, in Paul's words, we must seek to share our lives. We need to develop a habit of evaluating our priorities, and we need to recognize that the tasks we think are so critical are not more important than the people God has entrusted to us.

The life of Jesus furnishes powerful evidence of the importance of persons in the kingdom of God. The incident described in Mark 6:30–46 illustrates how Jesus managed the tension between task orientation and person orientation. The story opens with the account of a schedule so filled with needy people that Jesus and his disciples did not even have time to eat (v. 31).

Let us try to imagine the emotions Jesus felt. He and his disciples were obviously overwhelmed by work. He had recently been rejected by the people in his hometown (Mark 6:1–6). He may also have felt threatened by Herod (see Luke 9:9). He needed time to rest and to be alone to pour out his frustration to his Father over an unbelieving hometown and an evil king who had murdered John the Baptist, who was both herald of and kinsman to Jesus. In his place, most of us would probably have said to the crowd, "Can't you leave me alone for a while? I must have some time to myself. I need to think and pray."

Mark tells us, however, that when Jesus saw the large crowd, he did not engage in self-pity but "had compassion on them, because they were like sheep without a shepherd" (v. 34). Apparently this was not just a "whistlestop" visit either, for the text says that "late in the day" the disciples came to him and urged him to send the people away to the villages so that they might find food. Jesus again showed his compassion (and his power) by feeding all the people who had followed him (the number of the men alone was five thousand). Finally, after he had taught and fed them, he returned to his first objective, which was to seek solitude and prayer. He sent the disciples away in a boat, dismissed the crowd, and then "went into the hills to pray."

This story powerfully teaches that no goal or task is of greater importance than the people to whom God has sent us to minister. Jesus achieved his goal, but the time he gave to himself was from dark until the hours just before dawn (Mark 6:48). He gave the people to whom he ministered the best hours of his day; he served them in the hour of their need. This pattern occurs throughout the Gospels as time and again Jesus gives priority to a person in need instead of to his own tasks and goals. Consider, for example, the data in table 7, which shows that in Luke 4–9, Jesus on sixteen occasions gives priority to people in need and on only four occasions to a principle or task to be performed.

Table 7

Jesus' Priorities in Luke 4–9

Task or Principle	People
1. Declaration that no prophet is accepted in his hometown (4:24–30)	1. Healing of the sick and demon-possessed (4:31–41)
2. Declaration that he must preach to other towns (4:43)	2. The call to Simon to be a fisher of men (5:1–11)
3. Refusal to see his mother and brothers—declaration that those who hear his word and practice it are his true family (8:19–21)	3. Healing of a leper (5:12–14)
	4. Healing and forgiveness of a paralytic (5:17–25)
4. Settlement of the argument as to who is greatest—whoever is least (9:46–48)	5. Eating with sinners (5:29–32)
	6. Statement that as guests of the bridegroom the disciples need not fast (5:33–35)
	7. Picking grain on the Sabbath (6:1–5)
	8. Healing on the Sabbath (6:6–11)
	9. Healing of the centurion's servant (7:1–10)
	10. Raising of the widow's son (7:11–15)
	11. Forgiveness of the sinful woman (7:36–50)
	12. Healing of a demon-possessed man (8:26–39)
	13. Raising of Jairus's daughter and healing of a chronically ill woman (8:40–56)
	14. Feeding of five thousand (9:10–17)
	15. Healing of a demon-possessed boy (9:37–43)
	16. Refusal to curse hostile Samaritans (9:51–56)

Mark 6 and many other texts show Jesus meeting personal needs at whatever time they occurred; he delayed all other tasks until these needs had been met. This principle is of critical importance to western time-oriented missionaries. The Christian who is both task-oriented and time-oriented rarely has time for personal ministry. A classic example is a missionary couple I observed on a Navaho reservation. They were so frustrated that the Indians came with needs or demands at any time, day or night, that they refused to answer the door except during a three-hour period each afternoon. Navaho people told me that this couple had little interest in them personally; the missionaries' only concern was to have a good attendance at their worship services.

We cannot hold office hours for the people to whom Christ has called us to minister. We must adjust our time schedules, meeting them whenever they have need and turning to our own tasks only after we have completed our ministry to them, for Paul tells us in Colossians 3:12 that we are to clothe ourselves "with compassion, kindness, humility, gentleness and patience."

Incarnation in Another Culture

Clearly, the evidence from the life of Jesus shows us that people should take priority over task in ministry. Jesus consistently placed the needs of people ahead of task goals (table 7). Figure 2 depicts the tension between person orientation and task orientation. We may hypothesize that Yapese culture falls at (6,3) on the matrix, with high priority for persons and moderate priority for tasks, whereas American culture might be plotted at (3,6), with moderate priority for persons and high priority for tasks. We may hypothesize that the life of Christ falls at (7,4) on the matrix, for he gave perfect attention to persons and did the tasks that were essential. In Mark 6, Jesus set aside his private tasks for the sake of people in need; he returned to his tasks only after those needs had been met.

As Christians we are challenged to "be imitators of God, therefore, as dearly loved children and live a life of love, just as Christ loved us and gave himself up for us as a fragrant offering and sacrifice to God" (Eph. 5:1–2). We cannot accept the challenge of missions and ignore this admonition from Paul. Our aim should be that of Christ, a goal toward which we strive yet cannot attain except as his Spirit enables us. We should strive to give persons the highest priority (7,4) and balance the essential tasks.

Although we cannot reach perfection, we still can strive for the lesser goal of becoming incarnate in the culture of those we serve. If we are working with person-oriented Micronesians, then we must certainly give persons top priority in our

Figure 2

Values Assigned to Task and Person

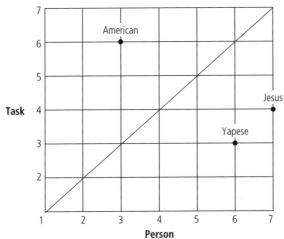

thinking. On the other hand, if we are working with Chinese or Japanese, who place great value on achievement, an orientation to people at the expense of productivity in our tasks may win us friends but may also lead to disrespect. In these cultures, person-oriented missionaries must give higher priority to accomplishing appropriate tasks. In essence, we need to move from a position comfortable to us and our culture to a position approximating the goals of the culture to which we are sent. Wherever we serve, our objective should be to live in such a way that we respect, love, and share our very lives (including our priorities and goals) with those to whom we seek to minister.

seven

Tensions
about Self-Worth

When my family was on Yap in 1980, our daughter Jennifer washed her blue jeans late one afternoon and hung them on the line. About seven that evening she went out to see if they were dry and discovered that they were gone. The clothespins were still on the line, but the jeans were gone. She came storming into the house, demanding, "Who took my jeans?" None of us had any clues.

The next morning we visited our Yapese neighbor and related the story of the missing jeans. Without hesitation she said, "Catalina—Catalina is the one who took them." We asked, "How do you know?" She replied, "Catalina goes home past your house every night, and she's a thief." We were not convinced by this bit of character assessment, demanding evidence that from our perspective was more substantial.

That same evening we were in the town of Colonia and attended a basketball game in which the high school boys from our municipality were playing. Catalina was also there, dressed in a pair of jeans that fit her perfectly. She was about four inches shorter than Jennifer and quite a bit smaller, but her jeans had a telltale green ink stain on the back of one pocket—right where Jennifer had once sat on a pen. Jennifer's jeans had apparently been cut down and sewed back together and were now a nice fit for Catalina. By this time the story of Jennifer's jeans had circulated widely, and several girls sarcastically asked Catalina where she had found them. Later that evening people in the village admired her new jeans, subtly indicating that they knew where she had obtained them.

The sequel to this story occurred about a week later when I was interviewing a woman fifteen miles away in southern Yap. After the interview itself and just as a matter of conversation, I told her the story of the jeans. Unable to picture Catalina, she asked who her mother was. When I answered, "Tinan," her eyes brightened in a flash of insight. She burst out, "Oh, that explains the whole thing. Tinan is a thief, so Catalina would be a thief."

When the Yapese ask who someone is, they want to know who the person's mother and father are, because they believe that one's character closely resembles that of one's parents. Identity, personal prestige, and worth are determined on the basis of birth. Family background is more important than personal accomplishments (or lack thereof).

Status Focus

Yap is a status-focused society, what Marvin Mayers categorizes as prestige-ascribed. Cultures and individuals with this orientation are concerned primarily with a person's birth and social rank. Respect is given to individuals on the basis of their social position.

Another example of this orientation is found in the Gospel of Luke. Apparently, in the Jewish culture of Jesus' day, prestige was assigned to a person rather than achieved. Luke opens his narrative with a detailed description of the family background of John the Baptist and Jesus and includes a complete genealogy of Jesus in chapter 3. Throughout the Gospel, we find references to prominent Pharisees and doctors of the law. These men were given places of honor at weddings and religious festivals (Luke 14). Their prestige apparently derived from (1) their genealogical heritage, (2) their membership in the leading religious societies, which involved rigorous training in the Jewish Scriptures and law, and (3) their inclusion among the prominent ruling families of Judea, who intermarried with one another and controlled considerable wealth.

Most individuals who find their basic identity and self-worth in the prestige ascribed to them enjoy playing the role assigned to their particular position in society. They relish the titles bestowed upon them such as Reverend or Doctor or Rabbi. They derive satisfaction from public rituals in which their particular position is formally honored. To sit at the speaker's table at a banquet is a contemporary example, while the seat of honor referred to in Luke 14 was a common means of recognition in first-century Jewish culture.

Further, such individuals prefer the company of their equals and shun or minimize contacts with those perceived as inferior. In the Gospels, Jewish leaders remark time and again about Jesus' persistent habit of associating and eating with the lower elements of society, namely, publicans and sinners (Luke 15:1–2). This behavior not only annoyed them but also caused them to question the legitimacy of Jesus' status as Rabbi. In American society, this same pattern is manifested when people buy homes in neighborhoods or join country clubs or particular church denominations that reflect their ascribed prestige. People who refuse, as Jesus did, to play their role in the prescribed way become outsiders in the social system and may be denied rights, privileges, and promotions by those in control.

Achievement Focus

In other cultures, prestige is not ascribed on the basis of social rank but is achieved. In societies with this orientation, an individual's identity and self-worth are bound up with personal performance. The dominant question is what the individual has accomplished. People with this value orientation scoff at titles and formal rituals of recognition. For them, success is the measure of their worth. This success may be defined in many ways. Some seek it in economic terms, measuring achievement by accumulation of property, income, and net worth. Jesus gives an illustration in the parable of the rich fool (Luke 12:13–21). Others seek success in the moral quality of their life and measure achievement in terms of personal righteousness. An example is the ruler who claimed to have lived a good life, having kept the commandments since he was a boy (Luke 18:18–30). Still others strive to achieve through a life of service, doing good deeds for family, church, or community.

In cultures in which prestige is ascribed, such prestige tends to be permanent. Not so in cultures in which prestige must be achieved. Athletes are praised for their recent performances but are quickly forgotten when someone younger surpasses them. Businessmen are lauded for their latest deal, but they become the object of condescending whispers when they fail to continue to succeed. Writers are praised or damned for their latest book, or lack of one, and so on. Respect is given to success that is current and continuing. Consider the Corinthians' treatment of Paul. It seems that a faction praised Apollos, who ministered among them after Paul and impressed them regularly with his oratory, so that they lowered their estimation of Paul, who, after his original success with them, had disappeared from the scene and had failed to return as promised.

People who have achieved prestige often develop a highly critical attitude toward themselves and others. They are seldom satisfied with their own achievements and struggle continually to do more. They quickly forget past achievements and strive to accomplish new goals. Like Martha (Luke 10:38–42), they look at others who are doing less than they are and judge them inadequate or lazy. This critical outlook may produce both deep envy and low self-esteem in those less gifted than others. On the other hand, it drives the successful to pursue higher and higher goals and to scorn those whose talents are less than their own.

Achievers enjoy and respect other achievers. They do not pay attention to family heritage or personal rank. Apollos, a Jewish disciple of John the Baptist, was accepted readily by the new Greek Christians (Acts 18:24–28) because of his achievements in knowledge of the Scriptures and his powerful ability to expound that knowledge. Americans, too, love successful people. Johnny Carson produced one of the longest-running shows on television by building it around interviews of successful people from all aspects of contemporary life. The versatile, the proficient, and the expert delight in diverse associates who, like Carson's guests, stem from different family, ethnic, and religious backgrounds and from every walk of life. The common basis for their interaction are their accomplishments and their mutual respect for others who are achievers.

Table 8

Status and Achievement Focuses

Status Focus (Prestige Is Ascribed)	Achievement Focus (Prestige Is Attained)
1. Personal identity is determined by formal credentials of birth and rank	1. Personal identity is determined by one's achievements
2. The amount of respect one receives is permanently fixed; attention focuses on those with high social status in spite of any personal failings they have	2. The amount of respect one receives varies with one's accomplishments and failures; attention focuses on personal performance
3. An individual is expected to play his or her role and to sacrifice to attain higher rank	3. An individual is extremely self-critical and makes sacrifices in order to accomplish ever greater deeds
4. People associate only with their social equals	4. People associate with those of equal accomplishments regardless of background

The Biblical Perspective on Human Conceptions of Self-Worth

It is imperative that cross-cultural workers be aware of their own conception of the basis of personal identity and self-worth. Then they must determine the attitude of their adopted culture on the same issue. Table 8 summarizes the two basic orientations: (1) status focus—prestige is ascribed on the basis of family background and social standing; (2) achievement focus—prestige is acquired through recent accomplishments. You may be surprised to learn that Jesus rejects both orientations as inadequate.

Jesus rebukes those who find their self-esteem in ascribed rank and public honors. In Luke 14:7–11, he warns those who seek places of honor that their self-aggrandizing will end in humiliation. He admonishes them to take the low places rather than the high.

A common practice then and now is entertaining guests in one's home. Jesus advises against inviting only our friends, relatives, and people of our own social class, occupation, and neighborhood (v. 12). How many of us who are middle class and financially secure actually live among the poor or even invite to dinner the common people to whom we minister? Most of the mission compounds I have visited in the third world have reflected a standard of living equal to the highest level of their particular society. In these compounds, the poor have not been the guests; rather, they have been the servants. But Jesus commands us to make the poor our guests of honor (vv. 13–14).

In Luke 14:26, Jesus strikes at the heart of Jewish social tradition. The prestige afforded by a noble ancestry, the honor attained by making an advantageous marriage, and the wealth and power gained from membership in a prominent family were the hallmarks of worldly success for Jews. When Jesus said to the crowd, "If anyone comes to me and does not hate his father and mother, his wife and children, his brothers and sisters—yes, even his own life—he cannot be my disciple," he repudiated the fundamental assumptions of their social life.

In striking contrast, the career Jesus prescribes for his followers is one of service. In Matthew 20:25–27, Jesus says that anyone aspiring to leadership in his service must be a servant, and the person aspiring to the top position must be a slave to the others. Paul tells us in Philippians 2:5–7 that Jesus himself set the example: "Being in very nature God . . . [he] made himself nothing, taking the very nature of a servant."

Individuals whose lifestyle reflects prestige ascribed to them because of their social position find servanthood a very uncomfortable career. Such people tend to rationalize their standard of living and have good arguments for maintaining the mission compound or for living in a culturally homogeneous suburb. They are probably so busy with the requirements of living their role that they have no time to entertain the poor as guests; the poor may even become their servants. It is extremely difficult for such people to become doers of the Word and not just hearers.

Others, however, take pride instead in their accomplishments. They may be like Martha (Luke 10), engaged in perpetual service to Christ, or like the rich young ruler who could say that he had kept all the commandments (Luke 18). They perhaps have a selfish need to do good and be good and look down on those who fall short of their performance.

The rich young ruler said to Jesus, "All these [commandments] I have kept since I was a boy" (Luke 18:21). He knew the rules, and he was an achiever, living the righteous life according to all the standards of his culture. How many missionaries and Christian workers are like this, confidently fulfilling their standards of righteousness and being seemingly flawless in their daily lives? Even though they may acknowledge their sinfulness in God's sight, their lives seem exemplary in contrast to the sin around them.

To the rich young ruler Jesus gave a simple command: "Sell everything you have and give to the poor. . . . Then come, follow me" (v. 22). Jesus asked of him something that was impossible for him to do. We often fail to see how this command applies to us, but Jesus' disciples saw its clear implication. They asked, "Who then can be saved?" (v. 26). They realized that Jesus was asking the impossible of all of us. If we have not sold all that we have, given it to the poor, and followed Jesus, we have not done enough!

Yet we continue to seek self-worth through our performance. Like Martha, we become evaluators of the less than perfect people who live and work with us. We look down on the inefficient, lazy, wasteful, and carnal national Christians who do not take care of the mission property, who steal from us (the wealthy), who lie to us to please us (the powerful), and when compared with us (the righteous), are less than exemplary morally.

Jesus rebukes Martha, saying, "Martha, Martha, . . . you are worried and upset about many things, but only one thing is needed" (Luke 10:41–42). Jesus does not say in this text what that one thing is. Rather, he says that Mary "has chosen what is better" (v. 42)—she sat at the Lord's feet and listened to his words (v. 39). People who think they can attain true self-worth through their accomplishments should bear in mind what Jesus says in Luke 14:26: Unless one hates "even his own life—he cannot be my disciple."

True Self-Worth

We feel a sense of self-worth when prestige is ascribed to us because of our social position or when we think we have achieved prestige through our accomplishments. Each culture defines its own paths to recognition and self-fulfillment. Yet this pursuit of prestige stands in opposition to the career of servanthood that God has for missionaries and for all believers.

The biblical estimate of self-worth is summed up in Romans 3:10–12: "There is no one righteous, not even one; there is no one who understands, no one who seeks God. All have turned away, they have together become worthless; there is no one who does good, not even one." In spite of the fact that many Christians know this text by heart, very few take it seriously in evaluating their own self-worth. Rather, we continually measure our performance vis-à-vis that of others around us.

However, in spite of our inherent worthlessness and empty self-righteousness, God finds worth in us. The parable of the lost sheep in Luke 15 emphasizes the longing that God has to bring us to himself and the joy that fills heaven when we repent from our self-directed way. Repentance, however, does not make us worthy; rather, it opens us to receive the gift of worthiness from God. Paul explains in Romans 3:21–24, "Now a righteousness from God, apart from law, has been made known." This is not a self-worth that can be obtained by human effort. "This righteousness from God comes through faith in Jesus Christ to all who believe. There is no difference, for all have sinned and fall short of the glory of God, and are justified freely by his grace through the redemption that came by Christ Jesus." Furthermore, whereas human attempts to find identity and self-worth divide us from one another and result in humiliation and subjugation of the weak, the gift of God's worthiness creates within us the servant attitude of Jesus, even to the point of giving our lives for others (Phil. 2:5–8).

The missionary, then, has to recognize that self-worth comes through neither ascribed nor achieved prestige and that one must be a servant in the pattern set by Christ. Yet the practical requirements of day-to-day living compel us to acknowledge and respect the cultural standards around us. Indeed, Paul reminds us in Titus 3:1–2 that servanthood requires that we be subject to rulers, authorities, and social norms (this, of course, reflects the standards of a culture in which prestige is ascribed). And at the same time he stresses that those who have trusted God must "be careful to devote themselves to doing what is good" (v. 8; a reflection of the standards of a culture in which prestige is achieved). To live a life consistent with the self-worth we have in God, we must be sensitive both to who we (and others) are and to what we do.

eight

Tensions Regarding Vulnerability

I was watching a baseball game in 1967 on the island of Yap, not suspecting that I was about to have a lesson in Micronesian culture. During the third inning, one of the teams had a hitting streak and kept scoring runs. As the twelfth run crossed the plate, the pitcher threw down his glove and walked off the field. His teammates, expressing the same frustration, gathered their equipment and left for home. The game thus ended abruptly as the team in the field, humiliated by the high score, thought it fruitless to play any longer. I was amused at this behavior but did not understand its full significance until later.

A similar incident occurred on United Nations Day, October 24. On Yap, this day was always a cause for celebration. People gathered from all the municipalities on the island to engage in various athletic and cultural activities. The foot races were particularly interesting to watch, since each area entered its best runners, and the spectators cheered on their local favorites with great excitement. I noticed that in one race after another, the lead runners looked back as they ran. Knowing that this slowed them down, I asked some Yapese for an explanation and received an unexpected answer. The Yapese runners were worried not that someone would catch them but rather that they would get too far ahead. If their lead became too great, the others would quit and walk off the course, and the leader would cross the finish line alone. The spectators would then ridicule the winner for showing off and embarrassing the others. To be too good was much worse than being not quite good enough. One must be concerned about the vulnerability of others.

Concealment of Vulnerability

Marvin Mayers (1982) characterizes Yapese society as a culture that perceives vulnerability as weakness. Individuals and cultures with this perspective try to avoid failure and error at all cost. The racer who runs far ahead makes the other runners look weak by comparison. A Yapese would rather not run than appear inept. The same pattern applies in other contexts. A Micronesian student would rather not take an exam than take it and fail or would prefer not to turn in a written assignment than demonstrate an inability to write. The Yapese simply do not want to make mistakes, and when they do, they try very hard to cover up their errors or to excuse them.

The achiever is a threat to those who are less competent. The American teacher who makes the mistake of publicly praising a Micronesian student has sentenced that student to such severe peer criticism that the student may purposely fail in his or her work for weeks to come. The A student is seen as showing off, making the others look bad. The peer group resents such insensitive behavior, which exposes the shortcomings of others.

Persons who feel that failure and vulnerability are weaknesses also strongly defend their positions and behavior. They feel threatened by anyone who disagrees with their point of view and are quick to assert that the others are in error and to deny any mistakes on their own part. It is essential for them to be right about an issue and to point out that others are wrong. Anything new or unusual is immediately suspect because it is not part of their experience and opens them to uncertainty. They do not like to enter new situations or take part in unfamiliar activities; such events produce anxiety for them, since the unknown context does not allow them to control their performance and thus to conceal their vulnerability.

Willingness to Expose Vulnerability

Americans, by contrast, often demand that people expose their vulnerability and risk failure. In sports, for example, Americans insist that games be played to the end, regardless of the point spread. Baseball games must go the full number of innings, even if one team is twenty runs ahead. Football must be played the full sixty minutes, even if the score is 74-0. The losing team is admonished to endure, to complete the game with as much dignity as possible. The important thing in American competition is completion of an event—did we finish the race, endure to the bitter end? Endurance, even in defeat, is evidence of personal strength in failure.

Quitters or those who refuse to push themselves beyond their own limits are scorned in American society. On the other hand, individuals who can laugh at themselves, joke about their failure, and jump back into the thick of a contest win admiration and respect. The most successful sports heroes do not allow failure to depress or paralyze them but bounce back with new strength.

Persons who are willing to expose their vulnerability are relatively unconcerned with error, either in themselves or in others. They enjoy learning from others, even when it puts their own weakness on display. In argument or debate, they can readily entertain a view other than their own and are open to criticism and suggestions from others. They are generally willing to try new ways of solving old problems or to explore areas that are unknown or untried.

Table 9

Concealment of Vulnerability versus Willingness to Expose Vulnerability

Concealment of Vulnerability	Willingness to Expose Vulnerability
1. Protection of self-image at all cost; avoidance of error and failure	1. Relative unconcern about error and failure
2. Emphasis on the quality of performance	2. Emphasis on completion of event
3. Reluctance to go beyond one's recognized limits or to enter the unknown	3. Willingness to push beyond one's limits and enter the unknown
4. Denial of culpability; withdrawal from activities in order to hide weaknesses and shortcomings	4. Ready admission of culpability, weaknesses, and shortcomings
5. Refusal to entertain alternative views or accept criticism	5. Openness to alternative views and criticism
6. Vagueness regarding personal life	6. Willingness to talk freely about personal life

The Biblical Perspective

A careful examination of New Testament teaching shows that each of these orientations—the hiding and exposing of vulnerability—has both positive and negative aspects. In Luke 14, Jesus teaches that there is wisdom in guarding one's weaknesses. Using examples of a man who wants to build a tower and a king who is about to go to war, Jesus commends estimating the cost and weighing one's vulnerability (vv. 28–33). To fail to consider one's weakness is foolish and opens one to public ridicule and error. To see vulnerability as weakness, then, is a wise thing. Jesus challenges his followers to choose the path of humility, which ultimately leads to honor (vv. 10–11).

At the same time, this value orientation contains pitfalls. The frequent dialog between Jesus and the Jewish leaders provides many illustrations, one of which is a reluctance to grapple with difficult questions. When Jesus asked them if it was lawful to heal on the Sabbath, they refused to answer (vv. 3–4). They did not want to discuss an issue that raised questions about the validity of their theological and practical position.

Another pitfall is a propensity to argue persistently for one's interpretation of an issue. The argument that the Sadducees presented in Luke 20 against the resurrection was an attempt to confound Jesus and to justify their own position. When he refuted them, they stopped asking questions (v. 40) but did not change their minds. The ultimate danger in such behavior is the covering up of errors and the denial of mistakes. When the Jewish leaders challenged Jesus' authority, his response caught them in their vulnerability (Luke 20:1–8). When he asked them about the authority of John's baptism, he ensnared them in a dilemma: "If we say, 'From heaven,' he will ask, 'Why didn't you believe him?' But if we say, 'From men,' all the people will stone us, because they are persuaded that John was a prophet" (vv. 5–6). So they answered simply, "We don't know," a refusal to admit the shakiness of their position.

Scripture is filled with paradoxes. Among them is its teaching regarding the issue under discussion, for while Jesus clearly taught that there is wisdom in taking one's vulnerability into account and guarding against failure, we also find that there is wisdom in accepting and exposing one's weaknesses. This is particularly evident in the writings of the apostle Paul. Focusing on his own life experience (2 Cor. 12:7–10), Paul writes that recognition of one's weaknesses results in dependence on God and his power. "That is why, for Christ's sake, I delight in weaknesses, in insults, in hardships, in persecutions, in difficulties. For when I am weak, then I am strong" (v. 10).

Paul argues that vulnerability is potentially a great source of strength to a believer. Just as Christ was crucified in weakness yet lives by God's power, so believers "are weak in him, yet by God's power . . . will live with him to serve you" (2 Cor. 13:4). Personal vulnerability also helps us find strengths in others. Paul says he is glad when he is weak but others are strong, and he prays for their perfection (v. 9). To accept one's vulnerability is to be open to the strength and support of others. Further, seeing weakness as an opportunity to impart strength prompts one to build up others rather than tear them down. All too often people see weakness and failure in the church as something to be destroyed. Paul not only accepted weakness in himself and others but also wrote to the Corinthians that the Lord had given him authority "for building you up, not for tearing you down" (v. 10).

On the other hand, a society that encourages a willingness to expose one's vulnerability and to risk failures is subject to the pitfalls of self-righteousness. By exposing the weaknesses of others, we may develop a condescending attitude toward them. Some of the Corinthian Christians saw Paul's public speaking ability as less than impressive and looked down on him for this weakness (2 Cor. 10:10–12). A related danger is that of developing a critical attitude toward those who do not see things our way. The factions that developed in the Corinthian church between the followers of Paul and those of Apollos were the result of such attitudes (1 Cor. 3:4). The greatest danger is that of self-centered arrogance, a casual and careless attitude concerning the weaknesses and failures of oneself and others (1 Cor. 4:18–5:2). Whereas accepting one's weaknesses should lead to dependence on the power of God, it may, if one focuses on self rather than on God, result in a casual attitude toward sin.

It should be evident from the discussion above that no biblical mandate supports one of these value orientations to the exclusion of the other. Neither pattern of behavior has the unqualified blessing of God. Both can be used for good or evil. For example, people who fear exposing their vulnerability may exercise wisdom and care in planning so that they do not overextend their resources, and they may show concern and sensitivity regarding the weaknesses and needs of others. At the same time, such people may deny their own vulnerability, cover up errors, and defend their position with an uncompromising fervor that on the surface is godly but underneath is nothing more than self-protecting. Some will refuse to admit a mistake, even though doing so might save others from trouble and conflict.

On the other hand, those who risk themselves feel free to expose the weaknesses in their personal lives and do not worry unduly about making mistakes or failing. However, if they expose errors in a society such as that of the Yapese, in which great anxiety surrounds mistakes, their behavior is cruel and hurtful. There is also the danger that personal freedom may develop into an attitude of condescension toward and criticism of others.

Further, a willingness to expose vulnerability may lead to carelessness in one's personal life and activities. One might, for example, make comments such as, "Why worry about that mistake? We all make them" or "You can't do great work all the time!" or "I don't care if things fall apart; you win some and you lose some." Such comments reflect an orientation to self rather than to others and a manipulation of values to serve selfish ends.

Avoiding Confrontation

During my research on Yap in 1979, I was faced with the unpleasant task of firing a Yapese man. He was part of a group being trained to administer an islandwide survey, and I discovered that he had made up the responses on survey forms he had returned to me. He was obviously having difficulty understanding my objectives, so I decided I could not employ him any longer.

Knowing that the Yapese generally cover up weaknesses, I determined to handle the matter as gently and as privately as possible, hoping to help the man save face and to maintain a positive relationship with him. I called him aside one afternoon, and as gently as I could, I told him he had lost the job. Because of the way I handled the situation and because I paid him for his work, which was of no use to me, I thought I had managed the situation in a generous and Christian manner.

To my chagrin the young man, while very polite, took the matter very hard. He had indeed lost face, and from that time on, no matter what I tried, he refused to have anything to do with me. If I had been interested only in my work, I could have dismissed the matter, but as a Christian I felt I had lost the opportunity to communicate the love of Christ to an unbeliever.

Some time later I experienced difficulty with another Yapese employee who was fabricating responses on the survey. Wanting to avoid, if possible, the alienation I had experienced with the first man, I asked a Yapese pastor friend for advice. Without hesitation he said, "Send somebody to talk to him." I was astounded. How could I do that? It was completely against my nature to take the cowardly way out. But my pastor friend persisted and persuaded me that it was the only way to handle the problem.

I asked one of the older men working for me if he would take my message of reprimand to the errant worker, and without hesitation he agreed to do so. We drove to the worker's village, where my colleague went alone to the man's home and in a very tactful but effective way told him of my frustrations with his work and of my intent to fire him if the problems were repeated. We then returned to the office and for a period of two weeks waited to see how the man would respond. When he returned to the office with a new batch of questionnaires, he greeted me as a long-lost friend. We engaged in warm and lively conversation, and our relationship appeared more solid than ever before. His work was not merely acceptable, it was excellent, and he became one of my most reliable and helpful employees.

I was puzzled as to why the second worker had responded so positively whereas the first man had rejected me so completely. My pastor friend explained the matter quite simply. On Yap, to tell a man to his face that he has failed is to treat him like an insignificant child. Sending a messenger to the second man meant that I considered him an equal or a superior and that I could not rebuke or expose his weakness to his face. He accepted the respect that my act of sending the messenger had shown him, and he returned that respect by giving me the quality of work he knew I desired from him.

This pattern of avoiding confrontation is characteristic of many non-western cultures. Mediators are essential in such cultures to build relationships or to repair the breaches that conflict has torn in the fabric of social relations. My American upbringing denies the validity of such mediation. As a leader I should accept the unpleasant obligation to reprimand in person. To send someone else is to abdicate my authority and responsibility.

The lesson of this case study is that we Americans must become incarnate in the cultures in which we minister. Many of my Christian friends protest, referring to Matthew 18:15, which says a person should show an offending brother his fault "just between the two of you." My answer is that the second Yapese worker did in fact see my message as being between the two of us exclusively. The use of a mediator was merely a means of delivering it in a way that showed my respect for him.

In Jewish culture also, private messages were often sent by intermediaries. Perhaps the most pertinent example is that of the centurion who asked Jesus to heal his servant. Matthew 8:5 reports that "a centurion came to [Jesus], asking for help." Luke 7:3 reports that "the centurion heard of Jesus and sent some elders of the Jews to him, asking him to come and heal his servant." The Gospel writers are not disagreeing with one another. The matter is simply a case like the one I described. The centurion did indeed come to Jesus, by way of mediators, to show that he felt Jesus was equal or superior to him. The text shows that he respected Jewish custom and did not ask Jesus to violate it by entering a Gentile's house.

As missionaries ministering in non-western cultures, we must be sensitive to the issue of vulnerability. Exposing the weaknesses of others by confrontation can destroy our witness and the evidence of the love of Christ in the gospel. We must relearn how to manage conflict and, when necessary, how to rebuke in gentleness and love. We might even learn to use mediation effectively to build the bonds of love and fellowship.

Vulnerability and Incarnation

We often fall into the trap of pursuing the ways in which our home cultures manage authority and conflict, even when those ways trample on others, wounding and alienating them from us. Paul shares with us in his letters a better way, the way of incarnation in the culture of the people we serve: "To the weak I became weak, to win the weak. I have become all things to all men so that by all possible means I might save some" (1 Cor. 9:22). His empathy with the people to whom he ministers is so great that he experiences in his own emotional and spiritual life their pain of weakness and their shame and sorrow at failure (2 Cor. 11:28–29). He charges us who are spiritual leaders and servants of Christ "to bear with the failings of the weak and not to please ourselves. Each of us should please his neighbor for his good, to build him up" (Rom. 15:1–2). Rather than pursue a course of critical evaluation of others and confrontation to punish them or coerce them into line, Paul calls us to love, affirmation, and empathy, not tolerating sin but embracing the sinner. The writer of Hebrews says that one qualification of a priest (or, we could add, of any spiritual leader) is that "he is able to deal gently with those who are ignorant and are going astray, since he himself is subject to weakness" (5:2). We must always be aware of our own weaknesses so we can remind ourselves to deal gently with the vulnerability of others.

Christian workers, then, must be aware of their perspective with regard to vulnerability, the predominant values of the culture in which they work, and the orientation of each individual to whom they must relate. They must be keenly aware of the potential of each orientation for building up or tearing down the body of Christ.

We must remember that God has chosen the weak (1 Cor. 1:27). This means that all those around us who regularly fail to meet our expectations are individuals God has chosen to do a job. It is our responsibility to work with them and to build them up (2 Cor. 13:10).

Perhaps even more important, we must recognize that we ourselves, and all of God's servants, will continue to be weak (1 Cor. 4:10). Our natural motivations are basically selfish, and our abilities are generally less than adequate to meet all the demands of a situation. Unless we are willing to accept this fact, we will continually fall into the traps of self-righteousness and condescension toward others. Jesus warns us to carefully consider our own weaknesses (Luke 14:28, 31) and to choose the path of humility (vv. 10–11).

Finally, we need to apply the principle that Paul gives us in Philippians 2:3–4: "Do nothing out of selfish ambition or vain conceit, but in humility consider others better than yourselves. Each of you should look not only to your own interests, but also to the interests of others." As we reflect on Yapese or Asian or African attitudes regarding competition and failure, we must be sensitive to the vulnerability of these people and not force our values on them. So often in our cultural arrogance we scoff at what we perceive as the weaknesses of those to whom we minister. Tragically, they in turn scoff at what they see as weaknesses in us. This attitude of vain conceit creates walls of rejection between us and greatly impairs the work of the body of Christ.

nine

Becoming 150-Percent Persons

Personal Values and Cultural Systems

Throughout this book, we have considered American culture as a collection of shared ideas and values, not all of which are held by each American. In fact, each person's value profile is unique, and there is often great variation among us in terms of our orientations. At the same time, we are all participants in a shared cultural community. These communities are made up of people, rules, regulations for behavior, structures that organize and coordinate social behavior, and structures that exclude some people and assign greater or lesser roles to members.

Each cultural community rewards individuals for certain kinds of behavior. Further, individuals are sometimes frustrated by their own culture, as when it puts pressure on them

113

to do things or behave in ways that are not natural or agreeable to them. A major purpose of culture is to coerce individuals to live together in society. It pressures people to submit to one another and to live together in a social framework. Yapese society, like all societies, is coercive, pressuring Yapese to live together under a common set of rules. And those rules, like ours, can be used for good or evil purposes. In the first edition of this book, I suggested that the system of culture was in itself neutral, but the people within the culture were moral or immoral. I no longer hold this position. I believe that the system of culture, like the people within the culture, is both moral and immoral.

In the Book of Romans, Paul speaks of people and communities as being controlled by the flesh. The flesh (*sarx* in Greek) is not merely an internal psychological sin nature, as it is translated in most contemporary English translations, but also refers to cultural standards with regard to circumcision, eating customs, observance of special religious days, and a whole host of regulations that were part of righteousness in Jewish culture and society. Paul concluded that Jews and Gentiles alike live in prisons of disobedience (Rom. 11:32), and he challenged his readers not to be conformed to their cultural standards but to be transformed by the renewing of their minds in Christ.

It is important then to recognize that culture, like language, is a powerful tool for communication and interaction. Scripture tells us that out of the same mouth come blessing and cursing (James 3:10). We can use the English language to bless someone or to curse someone. And cursing and blessing come not only from the individual heart but also from the standards and the customary practices of a social community. People often use the rules of a community to justify some forms of cursing and to condemn others. The standards we share are not merely personal but collective, and people are guilty of both personal and collective sin.

Paul draws a sharp contrast in Romans 8 between living "in the flesh" and living "in the spirit." In the ordinary state of human affairs, individuals and communities live in the flesh. Through the power of the gospel, people may be liberated from the bondage of the flesh, empowered to live as individuals and communities in the Spirit, and transformed by the power of the Lord Jesus Christ. In his letter to the Galatians, Paul challenges followers of Jesus to abandon a quest for righteousness achieved through the rules and regulations of their communities of the flesh and to follow Christ and live in the power of his Spirit. But he does not require Jews to abandon their culture. Instead, Paul argues that both Jews and Gentiles are prisoners of their ways of life and that God extends his mercy to both. God's mercy, through the death and resurrection of Jesus Christ, sets both Jews and Gentiles free from their laws of sin and death and enables them to fulfill the hope of their cultures through the righteousness of Jesus Christ. Vernon Sterk (1992, 47–51) suggests that God brings about transformational change in Jewish and Gentile cultures by affirming and fulfilling, through Christ, God's law and promise as they have been revealed and sustained in each.

When individuals and communities seek to follow Christ and live as he lived, their values and rules are transformed as people apply them in such a way as to honor him and to love others. Miroslav Volf (1996, 64–68) suggests that such a community embraces even its enemies and is characterized by forgiveness. In contrast, communities of the flesh exclude others, promote self-seeking and self-interest, and treat outsiders with disrespect and violence.

Culture in its complexity then is positive, negative, and sometimes neutral in regard to a relationship with Christ. For example, an individual who hides personal weakness and an individual who is willing to expose it may honor the Lord and love others, though they do so in different ways. And a person who regards prestige as a matter of social status and a person who sees it as a matter of achievement may submit their status or achievement concerns in humility to Jesus Christ and refrain from judging themselves or others. The keys for successful personal relationships in ministry are obedience to the commands of Scripture and accepting that others have a viewpoint that is as worthy of consideration as our own. Obedient Christians create communities of inclusion and embrace, to follow Volf. Such communities stand in contrast to the communities of exclusion and rejection that are typical in the world's cultures.

God's plan and purpose for us are that we be perfected in Christ Jesus and that we gather as his church, people, and communities filled with the Holy Spirit. As a result, ministering cross-culturally places special demands on us; we must, to paraphrase Paul, become all things to all people so that by all possible means we might win some (1 Cor. 9:22). As we live and interact with people of another culture, we must adapt to their ways.

Most Christian workers wonder how to define and identify sin in other cultural contexts. We must understand that sin is both personal and social, a complex interaction between individuals in a community. Sin may be individual, it may be collective, and it may be systemic within the structure of a community. Some Yapese use the status focus of their culture (prestige driven) to exert tremendous power over people or to destroy someone's reputation. These obviously evil actions flow from personal and collective motives. When individuals or groups do these things, they are usually supported by others in their community and engage in collective actions that are often destructive. However, other Yapese may use the same cultural values to build people up and to be generous and kind. The same value orientation may thus be used for good or evil.

It is important to understand then that the issues of time versus event, crisis versus noncrisis, or vulnerability concealed versus vulnerability exposed are not in themselves righteous or unrighteous. These value orientations are part of a more complex set of structures that are used either to exclude or to include, to embrace or to destroy. The structures of inclusion and exclusion and the will of the people employing them together result in individual and communal sin against others and against God.

Incarnation and Cultural Values

Attempting to belong to groups whose standards are in conflict with ours produces emotional stress within us and antagonism in our relationships with others. For this reason, most people choose to belong only to groups whose members have standards and values similar to their own. Our cultural prison is a comfortable place to be. Missionaries and others who accept the challenge of cross-cultural ministries, however, must, by the nature of their task, become personally immersed with peoples who are different. Following the example of Christ, that of incarnation, means undergoing drastic personal and social reorientation. As we observed in chapter 1, cross-cultural workers must be socialized all over again into a new cultural context. They must enter a culture as if they were children—helpless, dependent, and ignorant of everything from customs of eating and talking to patterns of work, play, and worship. And they must do this in the spirit of Christ.

The essence of the incarnation is entering the cultural prison of others and submitting to it for the sake of the gospel. For an adult, beginning over again as if a child can create great stress and emotional conflict. One must change patterns of thinking and living that have been developed over a lifetime. The purpose of the profile of basic values in chapter 2 is to help us assess our fundamental orientation and how it structures personal behavior and evaluation of the behavior of others. The profile furnishes a tool with which we can critically examine the role of underlying values in interpersonal relationships and conflicts.

Once we have an understanding of who we are, we must begin to investigate the values of others. Of course, it is often not possible to use questionnaires, and in some cultural situations, it would not be appropriate to do so. We must then carefully examine the behavior of those around us and try to form a profile of their personal and cultural values. Throughout this book I have hypothesized about the shared values of the Yapese people on the basis of what I observed of their lives and what individual Yapese told me regarding the motivations behind their actions. From this, I proposed that the Yapese people are holistic in their thinking and both event- and noncrisis-oriented. Individual Yapese vary in their personalities and the degree to which they conform to these orientations, but the shared culture does make certain specific demands of them.

To become incarnate in any culture, we must learn to adapt to it. To do so, we need to construct from our observations a hypothetical profile of its values and then compare our own values (our questionnaire responses) to that profile. From this comparison, we can identify areas in our value orientation in which we must adapt and change to be effective in our ministry. If, for example, we are strongly time-oriented, we will struggle in a culture that is just as strongly event-oriented. We must, if we are to become incarnate in such a culture, reassess and modify our values and behavior regarding time and schedules. We will need to develop new strategies for living. This reorientation will cause inner stress, and we will probably experience guilt and frustration over our failure to live up to the values instilled in us by our native culture. At issue, however, is the question of submission to God and his will for us to consider others better than ourselves and to yield to those to whom we minister.

In each segment of the profile of basic values, we will probably find differences, great or small, between our values and the values of those around us. The challenge is to accept differences in others and to walk from our own culture into the culture of others and to live their way rather than our own. This is not a simple task, for it requires a significant change in our pattern of learning. For most of our lives, we have learned within the given context of our native culture. We may never have questioned the context but assumed that it alone was the correct one. People in other cultures have learned in contexts that are defined differently. Therein lies the conflict. Before we can begin learning within a different culture, we must accept the change of context. We must believe that the new context is valid and potentially good. We must recognize that our understandings from our native culture are now inadequate, and we must begin to learn in the new context as children learn, yet with the speed and wisdom of adults.

150-Percent Persons

As conveyed in chapter 1, the goal of every missionary, and possibly every Christian, should be to become a 150-percent person. It is probably humanly impossible to become 100 percent incarnate in another culture. As finite human beings, we are constrained by the limitations of our minds, our life histories, and our personal abilities. Few of us have the emotional strength to endure the changes that full incarnation in another culture would require. We are weak people, yet God has made it clear that he loves the weak and uses them to accomplish his purposes. Therefore, the goal of becoming partially incarnate in the culture of those to whom we minister is, by God's grace, within our grasp.

We must begin the incarnation process by accepting without reservation the fact that God made us and that what he has done is good. Our life history, our personal trials and triumphs, our weaknesses and strengths are the materials that God is going to use to continue his creative work in us. If we do not accept the goodness of his past work in our lives, we will likely not trust his future work in us. Chronic self-rejection is the greatest barrier to becoming incarnate in another culture. If we do not accept as good God's shaping of our person and life in our own culture, we will never be able to accept his work in the lives of others who are culturally different from us.

The second step in incarnation is to accept the host culture as a valid, albeit imperfect, way of life. It is useful to remember that culture is basically a set of conceptual tools and social arrangements that people use to adapt to their environment and to order their lives in the pursuit of food, shelter, and family and community relationships. Each culture is the product of peculiar historical forces that have served to define a people's uniqueness in terms of personal and group identities. While every culture is imperfect and, in fact, a prison that holds people in bondage, each one is at the same time the integrating point of reference by which people comprehend themselves and others. We must understand that transforming a society does not mean moving people from their prison into ours but rather helping them to know Christ and be transformed personally and communally into people and communities of the Spirit. If we are to minister successfully to the members of a different society, therefore, we must learn about and participate in their culture.

It is important to remember that Jesus was fully incarnate in Jewish culture and life yet was without sin. Becoming incarnate in another culture does not demand or imply a loss of moral integrity. On the contrary, most missionaries who become genuinely incarnate in another culture experience a heightened sense of moral and ethical responsibility. They become aware of areas of sin in their lives to which their own cultural prison had previously blinded them. They also become conscious of legalistic attitudes and behaviors that before the cross-cultural experience had "an appearance of wisdom, with their self-imposed worship, their false humility" (Col. 2:23). Such persons now find that regulations by which they once lived are unable to restrain their carnal nature or to promote spiritual growth and maturity.

The key to growth and maturity in cross-cultural ministry is incarnation with complete submission to and dependence on God. When the Jews accused Jesus of breaking the Sabbath, of violating their communal norms, Jesus replied, "The Son can do nothing by himself; he can do only what he sees his

Father doing, because whatever the Father does the Son also does" (John 5:19). As Christians we are also children of God, and the Father is likewise our source of direction and power. Becoming incarnate in another culture will lead to sin only if we lose our sense of dependence on and unwavering trust in God and his Word. For all of us, the process of becoming incarnate involves becoming more than what we already are. In a real sense, it is another conversion. When we first believed that Jesus is the Christ, the Son of God incarnate in human flesh and blood, and that he was crucified and rose from the dead, we experienced a new creation in our lives. The Spirit of Christ came to dwell in us, and we experienced a reintegration of our whole person and life. We did not lose our original identity or our past life, but we entered into new relationships with both God and our fellow humans because of Christ's Spirit in us.

The first and most important step in what we might term "cross-cultural conversion" is recognition that culture defines the contexts for daily activities and relationships and that in the world there are hundreds of contexts, all of which are valid and useful to the people who share them. Once we have grasped this fact, we must take the more difficult step of acting on this belief. We must suspend our commitment to the context in which we have lived all our lives (at best a comfortable prison), enter into a cultural context that is strange to us (and a prison to them), and see that new context as the framework for our life and ministry. Peter speaks of this as being aliens or strangers in the culture to which God sends us. By doing so we will experience a reintegration in our lives, yet we will not lose our prior identity or personal culture and history. This significant change in our thinking will allow us to enter into relationships with people whose values and lifestyles are fundamentally different from our own.

The goal of this book has been to show that the incarnation of Christ is a powerful analogy for missionary and other Christian ministry. We have seen that he was both fully God and fully human. He entered the world as an infant and grew up in the culture and ways of life of first-century Jews. Jesus was a 200-percent person, fully God and fully human in the life and world of Jewish culture. Numerous Scripture passages demonstrate that Jesus' ministry among the Jews reflected and harmonized with their culture, and he commands us to follow his example. If we desire to be obedient to Jesus' command, to carry the good news of his resurrection to the world, we must be willing to become 150-percent persons. We must accept the value priorities of others. We must learn the definitions and rules of the context in which they live. We must adopt their patterns and procedures for working, playing, and worshiping. We must become incarnate in their culture and make them our family and friends. We must do all this empowered through faith and freedom in Jesus Christ and living in the Spirit and not in the flesh.

References

Brown, Raymond Edward, ed. 1970. *The Gospel according to John.* Anchor Bible. Garden City, N.Y.: Doubleday.

Carter, Rita. 1998. *Mapping the Mind.* Berkeley: University of California Press.

Conn, Harvie M. 1984. *Eternal Word and Changing Worlds: Theology, Anthropology, and Mission in Trialogue.* Grand Rapids: Zondervan.

Cook, Michael L. 1997. *Christology as Narrative Quest.* Collegeville, Minn.: Liturgical Press.

Gladwin, Thomas. 1970. *East Is a Big Bird: Navigation and Logic on Puluwat Atoll.* Cambridge: Harvard University Press.

Hall, Edward T. 1973. *The Silent Language.* Garden City, N.Y.: Doubleday.

———. 1976. *Beyond Culture.* Garden City, N.Y.: Doubleday.

Kraft, Charles H. 1983. *Communication Theory for Christian Witness.* Nashville: Abingdon.

Levinson, John R. 1999. *Of Two Minds: Ecstasy and Inspired Interpretations in the New Testament World.* N. Richland Hills, Tex.: BIBAL.

Loughlin, Gerard. 1996. *Telling God's Story: Bible, Church, and Narrative Theology.* Cambridge: Cambridge University Press.

Mayers, Marvin K. 1974. *Christianity Confronts Culture.* Grand Rapids: Zondervan.

————. 1982. Basic Values. A class syllabus at Biola University, La Mirada, Calif.

McConnell, William T. 1983. *The Gift of Time.* Downers Grove, Ill.: InterVarsity.

McFee, Malcolm. 1968. The 150-Percent Man: A Product of Blackfeet Acculturation. *American Anthropologist* 70: 1096–107.

Miller, J. V. 1983. The Time of the Crucifixion. *Journal of the Evangelical Theological Society* 26(2):157–66.

Paredes, Anthony J., and Marcus J. Hepburn. 1976. The Split Brain and the Culture-and-Cognition Paradox. *Current Anthropology* 17:121–27.

Sterk, Vernon Jay. 1992. *The Dynamics of Persecution.* Ph.D. diss., Fuller Theological Seminary.

Volf, Miroslav. 1996. *Exclusion and Embrace: A Theological Exploration of Identity, Otherness, and Reconciliation.* Nashville: Abingdon.

Index